PENBANC
Notes from a Welsh Farmhouse

Gaynor Funnell

Foreword by Jon Gower and Ali Anwar

Acknowledgements

With many thanks to Ali Anwar from the H'mm Foundation, creator of the Nigel Jenkins Literary Award, and without whom this book wouldn't be possible. Evie Spicer, my niece, for understanding the heart of Penbanc and taking her beautiful photographs accordingly. Gill Hailey for her kindness, and for helping edit the final draft of this book. All friends and family for their love and support at the most difficult of times. To fellow MA students and staff at Swansea University Creative Writing department. Your help and critique has been invaluable.
Kate and Anna, the new custodians of Penbanc, for becoming friends and allowing me to still visit.

Special thanks go to two people –
Jon Gower, a generous teacher and friend, who has been involved from the beginning of this book's story right up to its end. His support and knowledge has been invaluable.
My dear friend Carole Hailey, who started a writing group in Pembrokeshire, where I found a voice. She convinced me I could write and persuaded me to apply for a Masters in Creative Writing at Swansea. Her kindness and belief in my writing has never wavered, so this book has evolved from her willingness to share.

Acknowledgement is due to Nigel Jenkin's literary executors: Angharad Jenkins, Margot Morgan and Branwen Jenkins.
Also to the literary executors of: Edward Thomas, Roger Deakin, Ralph Waldo Emerson, Tim Dee, R.S. Thomas and Jan Morris.
Thank you to Moira Lloyd and Paul Spicer for their help in proofreading. And to Andy Dark for putting this volume together.

To Dave and our daughters

First published by The H'mm Foundation in 2023

© Gaynor Funnell

ISBN: 978-1-9999522-4-2

All rights reserved. No part of this publication may be reproduced, stored in a retrieval system or transmitted in any form, or by any means, electronic, mechanical. photocopying, recording or otherwise without the explicit permission of the publishers.

The rights of the contributors to be identified as authors of their contributions has been asserted in accordance with the Copyright, Design and Patents Act, 1988.

Photographs by Evie Spicer www.eviespicer.com
Typeset and designed by Andy Dark
Printed in Wales by Gwasg Gomer,
Llandysul Enterprise Park, Llandysul, SA44 4Jl

Published by the H'mm Foundation,
c/o Bevan Buckland, Langdon House, Langdon Road,
Swansea SA1 8QY.

Contents

- *2* Connections
- *6* Foreword
- *8* A Sense of Place
- *14* Snow, Christmas and Parc Penrhiw
- *22* Nests
- *32* A Suffragette Spring
- *38* A Place of Loss
- *46* An Oak and a Kite
- *52* What3Words
- *56* A Drift of Rock and Sea
- *60* The Witch's Cauldron
- *64* Gog and Magog
- *74* A Decision to Leave
- *80* A Beltane Walk
- *90* The Lane
- *98* The Rose
- *104* Cracks
- *108* Fields
- *112* Fields of Gold
- *118* How Far Can a Ladybird Fly?
- *122* Night
- *130* Perambulating
- *148* Barn Owl
- *152* Time in a Garden
- *162* Hedgehogs, Harvests and Moles
- *174* Conker
- *178* Fossils, Feathers and Stones
- *184* Leaving
- *191* Footsteps – A Footnote
- *192* Epilogue. Moving Forwards – A Day in a Life

~ *Connections* ~

*And how, in this place, worker of the word,
might you find yourself useful?*

(Nigel Jenkins)

In November 2022, I received a call from David Britton, director of Creative Writing at Swansea University, to tell me I'd been awarded the Nigel Jenkins Literary award. Unexpected, good news is always welcome, although good isn't the best word to describe my feelings. Emotional, surprised, excited – all of these and more. Maybe more so because my work was deep-felt, so personal. And like many writers, praise is something we often feel uncomfortable with, feel it's undeserved. Also, as I hadn't known there was to be an award, an award generously given by Ali Anwar, founder of the H'mm foundation and a good friend of Nigel Jenkins, it was even more of a surprise.

I'd read poems by Nigel before I was aware of who he was – poet, psychogeographer, teacher, and more. I had several of his books. Coming late to writing creatively, poetry was my first love and I became increasingly interested in haiku although knew nothing about it. A fan of second-hand books, I picked up a book *Another Country*, haiku poetry from Wales, by Nigel Jenkins, Ken Jones, and Lynne Rees. On the first page was one of Nigel's poems –

> *she introduces*
> *her baby to his shadow:*
> *he waves, it waves back*

This small arrangement of words crystallised to me how only a few words can convey a snapshot of a moment in time. I enjoyed his haibun, especially 'Willy Harry,' and used a technique of mixing prose and poetry together in some of my own essays.

In another second-hand copy, *Footsore on the Frontier*, 'To Sue, with best wishes', is scrawled in thick black pen across the page. One of my favourite essays in this book is 'Getting Old for Two', where he writes about the death of his father. Many of his words resonated and stuck with me and I remembered them when I was writing about my own grief, '…But with an afterlife in the memories of the living, the dead rarely leave us alone for long…'

For anyone who has read any of my own writing, they will know that punctuation is not my strongest point. Perhaps I should have read his Punctuation Poems before beginning to write, with descriptions of the hyphen, the dash, the apostrophe and more. Perhaps we should read these rather than dry, textbook explanations.

When I started my MA in Creative Writing at Swansea University in the department he helped to create, people spoke of Nigel with love and gratitude, as if he was still there. They talked of his generosity as a teacher, how he championed new writers. His spirit still strides the corridors to those that knew him. His influence continues, as without the award named after him, my book, *Penbanc*, would not have been published.

How difficult to choose my favourite works of Nigel's. Favourite poems, like favourite songs, change from month to month, even day to day. Apart from the works described above, the one's I've chosen resonate with the farm and the landscape, the heart of my own book, apart from *Watch*, which reminds me of my dad.

As I'm writing this, my sleeping grandchildren are curled like commas either side of me. Their grandfather comes from Baghdad, the same city as Ali Anwar, just another invisible thread. Sometimes real-life coincidences and connections can be stranger than fiction.

Gaynor Funnell

~ *Haiku* ~
(Nigel Jenkins)

frosty bark
as I squint the Pleiades
of fox, *cadno*, fox, fox

last year's leaves –
a bushy oak rustling
in icy winds.

Sunned earth fizzing
with rumours of barley
as the rain sinks home

plough and tractor
mobbed by gulls; the sheen
of bladed earth

the rains,
in breeze-rushed leaves,
transformed

~ *Foreword* ~

John Gower and Ali Anwar

It is possible to love a place so well that it becomes a part of us, its contours like those of our bodies, its grasses like the fine hairs growing out of our skin. You can see this evidenced in this fine book, where Gaynor Funnell maps out the fields and lines, the gates and lanes of a small farm in west Wales. When she and her husband Dave moved here they were following a dream and bringing with them a small menagerie of five dogs, three pet sheep, half a dozen chickens and a barn owl.

Penbanc: Notes from a Welsh Farmhouse is chock full of attentive writing about nature's presence whilst also being a careful consideration of grief and its absences. As Gaynor charts the slow but sometimes startling passage of the seasons and observes the wildlife and weather around her home in west Wales, she details a world of quotidian change, creating an intimate, revealing journal of long walks, the joys of standing still and of deep personal exploration of a house as it becomes a home.

Gaynor, a sublime writer about the patterns of nature and the shapes of the land, is very good on plants, be they the ones she planted in the farmhouse garden to catch the light and in some ways to make it apparent or those that nature seeded and spread. Take this Springtime example which is lyrical, sensual and very attentive: it offers ample evidence in itself of the calibre of the writing throughout:

Today, Spring is the colour purple. Purple, white and green. From my limited viewpoint out of the kitchen window, ribbons of violet, lavender, mauve, lilac, indigo and white crocus wander between a sward of fresh green. Their flowers arch from a cluster of thin, straplike leaves, which have a chalk-line drawn down the centre of them. A finger-touch of sun is all that's needed for the tulip-shaped flowers to open like sea anemones, their golden stamens trembling in the March breeze. One has caught a fat bumblebee. It has a tawny, chenille bottom and climbs lazily over the petals with sherbet-dusted legs, as if just woken from a soporific slumber.

You can both enjoy and dwell on the felicities of such writing, with its vivid sense of colour, its near-scientific level of detail in the description and the neat framing of the land as a chink of view from the kitchen window. We are there with her, enjoying the vernal display and its promise of lengthening days and more fat bumblebees. She is our trusty guide but also a most affable companion, as she tells us about days of snowfall, the swirl of red kites or the habits of sheep. She visits ancient cromlechs and appreciates the texture of conkers, takes us down hidden lanes and listens to the whispers of people who lived here long before she ever did. Gaynor, writing about Penbanc, does so with great love and highly-attuned attention, that attention being one precise way we can underline how we do indeed love a place so very well.

~ *A Sense of Place* ~

Why do some places hold you more than others? Why do some draw you in even if you've only been within their embrace for a short while, whilst others leave no mark when you've known them for years. And if there should be a house within such a familiar place, when does that house become a home? And where do the boundaries of a such a home begin and how far do they extend?

For me, home starts as soon as I pass through Glanrhyd – a hamlet 'on the side of the ford' – climb up the steep-sided hill where the banks are primrosed-yellow in spring and where the trees touch overhead so it feels like you're travelling through a tunnel, then turn right off the lane which heads downwards towards Moylegrove and Ceibwr Bay, and cross over the rattling threshold of the cattle grid, which leads down the track towards Penbanc – the house at the top of the bank. A head-high hedge of hazel, hawthorn, blackthorn and gorse runs down the first part, anchored in place with coils of ivy, bramble, and the apple-scented-leaves-after-rain sweet briar rose; just as the tumbledown barns and decaying gates downwind are held together with fistfuls of turquoise and orange hanks of baler twine. I know the hedge as well as I know the forget-me-not blue and white *toile de jouy* curtains that frame the upstairs window. The hedge gives way to open fields, dotted with angled trees. On some days you can see the distant glimmer of the sea, a pocket handkerchief sliver of Cardigan Bay, and where, on a clear night, the searchlight beam from the lighthouse at Strumble Head eerily sweeps the fields.

Penbanc lies at the end of the track, on the only level part of its surroundings. The geology and geography of the place leads to the building being exactly where it is – low enough for protection from the westerly winds and high enough to avoid the winter-flooding from the bottom fields. Its feet are embedded in the shale its walls are made from and its body is supported with the remains of long dead trees. A spring appearing magically from the fissures of the shale, provides it with dark-cold water. There are three small quarries on the land, and three dwellings to go with each one. One house lies broken and empty since its roof disappeared – it's returning to the land that made it.

My husband Dave and I moved here ten years ago, with five dogs, three pet sheep, half a dozen chickens and a barn owl. Then, Penbanc was a house, not yet a home.

It's not large and looks like a house a child might draw, with uneven, chalk white walls and a smoking chimney. It's not symmetrical – the 'eye' of the right-hand window droops downwards and bulges outwards, as if it's suffering from a facial palsy. The house needed a lot of work then – tell-tale dots of woodworm; water seeping through the kitchen floor after it rained, an interesting take on an indoor water feature; a crumbling chimney – so now I feel I know every intimate inch of it. The house faces the wrong way when you come down the track: you arrive at the back of the house, the so-called tradesman's entrance, whereas the front door – which no-one ever uses but is perfect for placing the Christmas tree against – peers out across the trees. But if you look closer, under the tangled curtain of sycamore and ash, and hidden by decades of soil and leaves and grass, is an old green lane. Hundreds of years ago, it was the main path leading from the cottages lying further down the valley to the nearby town of Cardigan, some four miles away along the metal road.

At right angles to the farmhouse and a border to the green lane is a converted barn which was once a stable and cowshed. It was meant to bring in income as a holiday cottage, and we lived there when the farmhouse was being renovated, but a succession of children have made it their home over the years. It now lies empty apart from its memories, and the cat, who sneaks in when he can.

In winter, looking northwards from Cromlech field, which lies north of the farmhouse, you can just make out the grey spire of Monnington church, which is about two miles away. Along with the churches in nearby Moylegrove and Bayvil, it's one of the local churches where some of the previous residents were laid to rest.

Parts of the house are very old. I have documents written on cracked and crinkled bone-hued parchment dating back to 1734, the black and red of the calligraphy still clear and readable, but the foundations of Penbanc, or Penbank, or Pen-y-banc, were here long before that. I know that the Rowlands, the Devonalds, the Biddyrs, the Williamses, the Lewises all lived here; that David Devonald was born here in 1783, that his son John, born on August 6th, 1815, killed a man during a fight at the annual Eglwyswrw Meigan fair, and had his sentence of hanging commuted to imprisonment in Australia. He sailed from Liverpool on October 6th, 1835, on *The Susan* and was released for good behaviour, eventually becoming mayor of a small town, before being killed on Christmas day in 1856 whilst saving a woman from being run over by a train.

Does knowing the names of these long-dead people and a little of their long-ago lives make me feel more at home? I think it does. It adds another layer to the sense of place, or my sense of place. There are other gentle reminders of those who have lived here before – children talking from a distance, someone leaning over a bed at night. I'm not as aware of them as I once was. Perhaps I've got used to them, or they've got used to me. I don't see them or the past as a barrier – more of a gateway, maybe.

There is a re-leaded stained-glass window leading into my bedroom which lets the light in and keeps the dark out. It's the colour of the palest Italian pistachio ice-cream, embraced by a Marian-blue border and it's the first thing I see in the morning and the last thing I see at night. For years, it reflected on the souls of a church in Swansea, until it was removed due to the church's deconsecration. Alan, our roofer, saved it whilst working there and kept it for years before bequeathing it to me. He also left his 'special mark' on part of our roof 'for protection', something he only did for people he liked, or so he said. We had to search to find it – a thumb sized image of a lion staring unblinkingly towards the north star.

Although the walls of the house are physical borders, my sense of home stretches further than the four wonky walls, the outside space being as familiar as the inside. I've spent years digging, planting, pruning, even crowbarring an inhospitable field to create a garden. The trick is to find the right plant for the right spot and leave it to get on with it. There is no room for 'soft' gardening in this harsh canvas. Over the years, I've planted over fifty roses, to weave through the trees and soften the slate landscape. They're mainly historic varieties with gloriously romantic names. I know some won't survive as the air is too clean and the soil lies too wet, but enough will.

Looking out of my kitchen window, a squat-trunked, badly pruned apple tree forms a visual border. It bears blush-yellow pear-shaped fruit in September that are just about edible – I leave them for the blackbirds. Next to it is a flowering cherry tree, which was planted by the previous owners over twenty years ago. They've moved on, but the cherry remains, resplendent with marshmallow blossom in the spring and flames of ochre, mustard and magenta in autumn. I hang birdfeeders from the lower branches and have to tip-toe through swathes of the tulip-shaped blooms of *Crocus tommasinianus*, the woodland crocus, which open like amethyst starfish in the sun, to reach them. Every year, the bulbs incrementally slide down the slope and every year I try to plant some elsewhere. They stubbornly refuse to thrive however – they know their place.

In Gwair field – the field in front of the trees which are the physical border of our land – lies the pumphouse for the spring that provides water to the sink I'm leaning against now. It also feeds the cottage next door, the barns and fields. I can just see it from the kitchen window. The pumphouse sits in a small man-made flattening in this land of slopes, and dips and hollows. Three children of the house used to play cricket here, and there are tales of one of their cricket bats 'twitching as if it had a life of its own' as they crossed the field where the pumphouse is now. It's the exact spot that a water diviner found the spring years later.

In the right-hand corner of my vision is an old railway carriage. There are many of them scattered amongst the nearby landscape and I presume they are the reminders of the local railways shutting down. I use it as a potting shed but more importantly, it houses swallows when they arrive, the wonky roof and walls, plus a nearby supply of mud making it a perfect nesting site.

I'd like to say I know the sky towards the west as much as I know the rest of my landscape, but I don't. Every day is different, and I don't possess enough words to describe adequately the sunsets of burnt umber, amber, coral, cerise and peach, the February days of woodpigeon-grey, pewter and pearl, and the crystalline pinholes of stars on a soft September evening. Last summer I sat outside, binoculars in hand, to try and spot Elon Musk's Starlink satellites. I saw them once – a necklace of tiny silver dots travelling from left to right against the inky sky. A different boundary being explored, rightly or wrongly. Technically, we all own the airspace above our properties: "Whoever owns the soil, holds title all the way up to the heavens and down to the depths of hell". Today that's limited to about 500 feet above apparently – another boundary, but an invisible one.

There's an invisible boundary inside the house now. Dave passed away in the front room eighteen months ago, and even though I've painted, carpeted, re-curtained, the room doesn't feel like home anymore, not yet. It's as if there's an invisible gate I have to pass through to walk into it, taking a mental and physical breath in before I do so. And mentioning him is another barrier to cross. He's added another layer to this house full of the land and its ghosts, and maybe the people that live here in the future will hear his voice with the others, swearing as he hits his head on another low beam.

~ *Snow, Christmas and Parc Penrhiw* ~

It snowed the first winter we were at Penbanc, thick, fat flakes that covered everything they touched within the hour. I'd smelt the coming snow in the air the day before it arrived, although none of my family believed smelling snow was a thing. Incoming snow has an unexplainable but unforgettable smell, with traces of raw-steel and damp-cold that made my nose twitch, and I'd take a deeper breath in, as if by absorbing more of the air, I could work out what snow really did smell like.

There's never any snow around here, we'd been told when we'd moved in. The weather was too mild; Penbanc was too near the sea; there was salt in the air. They were wrong. December 2010 would be the coldest in 100 years.

Snowfall started that afternoon, and by dusk, everything was disguised under a mantle of white. When I awoke the next morning, the oblong of light shadowing around the uneven edges of the bedroom window frame was brighter than normal, so I guessed the snow was still on the ground. Unusually for me, I got out of bed quickly and went outside, for once ignoring the cold.

I love snow, love the transformative power of it. Every sound lay hushed but my senses were on alert, open to this new landscape. The snow gave a different perspective to everything, and the hills seemed an almost touchable distance away under a lowering ceiling of gun-metal grey sky. And it was still snowing, the flakes falling silently, as weightless as dove feathers, settling on my coat, fading as they slowly melted. Snowflakes seem so insubstantial, so how do they manage to cover everything so quicky? One floated onto my finger and I brought it to my mouth to taste it – a fleeting ice-melt to nothingness.

It was eerily quiet with not a sound from the birds. No sign that any farmers were working. Across the fields, snow lay as frozen waves below the hedge line, piling in tints of blue pools around the gateposts. The snow squeaked and scrunched under my feet as I walked across the field and Bob, Gael, and Jim, the sheepdogs, flew around in circles, creating miniature snowstorms, the snow crystals sticking in clumps between their pads. One stopped mid-circle, biting and chewing this new white substance. At the top of the slope, a straight line of animal tracks led diagonally across the field; four toes plus a pad in a rough diamond shape meant this was the mark of a fox. The sheep huddled under the sycamore, their white fleeces of yesterday now dingy against the bright.

We followed the feetings downwards to where they disappeared into the shadows of the woods. The quietness persisted as we walked, the snow muffling every sound and keeping everything inwards. Even the dogs became quieter and followed close behind me. And though I already knew the woods were a magical place, the snow made them Narnia-esque; a keeper-of-secrets kind of place. Gone were the hillocks of dead grass, the fallen branches, the mounds of dead leaves, and instead was a white-out of curves and ski-runs with everything smoothed and rounded at the edges. Wedding cake icing tumbled from hedges and sugar crystals flurried from branches. Snow reduced the landscape to two colours only: black and white. Black sentinels of trees; a slow, peat black trickle of water in the stream; a filigree of black bramble, which the snow hasn't managed to touch. Everything else was painted Farrow and Ball paint shades of white; shadow, shaded, tallow. Deeper into the depths of the wood was an enclosed, liminal world, where the trees touched overhead, bending with the weight of the overnight snow. It was a special feeling to be the first being to step into and onto this new land.

Birds descended on the farm over the following days; vees of geese honking their way through the mist, lying low against the pearl-soft sky and the Teifi river; hordes of field-fares, redwings, mistle thrushes thronging and gorging on the frosted red of holly, rowan and hawthorn, until only denuded branches were left. Starlings chattered, nattered and swarmed, moving as one as they blackened the trees; red kite and buzzards quartered the bareness of the fields, the ground too frozen for even the buzzards to dig for worms, while the sparrowhawk, in shades of pewter grey and peach, cruised the bird table and the nearby hedge line.

Our daughters were supposed to be coming for Christmas, if the snow let them. I was so looking forward to seeing them, all of us being together in this new place. We'd had our own Christmas rituals in our old home, as families do. It would be interesting to see which ones persisted here, or what new ones might grow.

I couldn't sleep the night before they came, so went outside to quiet my mind. The night was almost as bright as a spring dawn because of the moonshine reflecting from the snow and silence lay all around like an embrace. I raised my head moonward to breathe in and absorb the just waning moon. Away from me, the shape of my boots lay as darkened patches against silver; visual evidence of the walk I'd done earlier, and I re-traced my footprints along this new path, stopping to lean against a gate, blowing onto my fingers to keep them warm. My moon-shadow loomed as I leant, different to a sun-shadow somehow. It stretched and bent at a different angle to my body and I waved at myself and to the spirits of the night and made owl-wing patterns with my fingers. The hedges and trees also seemed different in this cold light, perhaps they too found this new landscape unnerving. Almost on cue, a tawny owl called from the dark of the woods and called again as it flew silently along the green, now white lane. Its partner replied, the sound drifting and dispersing and echoing across the fields as I made my way back indoors to wait for the next day.

It was cold in the house. As the renovation of the farmhouse had yet to begin, there was no central heating, only wood burners and electric heaters. I hated feeling cold and I know the girls did too. I had a hot water bottle permanently attached to some part of me. The practical benefit of having our own wood meant there was plenty of firewood, the branches or trees just needed to be cut. Sorting out wood was one of Dave's favourite pastimes, so he'd spent the day before collecting, chopping and storing cut logs. The woodshed was the tidiest place on the farm, including the house. The hardwoods of oak and ash which were common on the farm were good for burning as they have a low water content; birch burns easily but fast so needed to be mixed with hardwoods; the hawthorn, holly and hazel also burn well. Oak is the wood that was used for Yule logs and kept for 12 nights after Christmas, not that we were intending to follow that tradition. We were lucky we had a lot of wood to burn. We needed it that winter.

For the first time in years we had a white Christmas. The snow lay like an expensive carpet over the ground – no fraying, no marking, no shrinking – and the low temperatures meant it stayed exactly where it was. We made a snowman and lay on the compacted, fallen snow and made snow angels. Even though we were adults the snow brought out the child in us all. It was the same temperature inside the house as outside and the fingertips of Jack Frost made psychedelic swirls of ferns and flowers on the inside of the windows every morning. We wore jumpers, and jumpers over the jumpers, and hats and scarves inside the house until the wood-burners and Raeburn sparked a temporary magic, filling the house with the smell of autumn.

It snowed again before the girls left and because none of the trains were running, Dave had to take them back to Sussex, which was normally a six-hour journey. It was strange to have the house to myself, a place quietened under a roof of snow, and just after I watched them leave, I realised there was no water. It came into the house via a bore hole, a fair distance away in Gwair field and the pump that made it usable was situated in one of the outbuildings. Somewhere along this line, the supply had become frozen meaning no water to the house or the barns. There was one tank only and that wouldn't last for long. In the pump shed, I exposed as much of the pipe as I could but realised I was never going to be able to defrost it all. The only thing to do was to melt some snow. I found the largest saucepan I had and piled it with snow, melting it on the Raeburn before filling up the animals' water bowls, something which had to be done a number of times over the next two days. Dave would have to fix the problem when he returned.

In the holding yard, icicles resembling rows of cold incisors hung from the corrugated iron roof and snow draped like cornices from the silage shed. The large metal water trough in the centre of the yard was solid ice, mercury air bubbles captured within it, and through the top the brown, frozen strands of the water lily stems stretched towards the snow-full sky. Against the barn, a rose, blush-pink and cream, left on the stem from a November flowering, was captured in an icy embrace, until its grip melted, leaving shattered petals which dropped at a touch.

I scraped away some of the snow on the concrete floor so I could leave seed out for the ground feeding birds. They soon came – robin, sparrow, blackbird, chaffinch, dunnock. I filled the fat ball and peanut feeders and would have to do so again in the afternoon as the birds were hungry. The snow may be beautiful but is no friend to them. I cracked a hole in the water trough for my sheep, gave melted snow to Magik the barn owl. In the ark that housed my silkie bantams, the snow in their outside run was as tall as they were so I left them inside. Silkies don't like getting wet. Silkies are from China, and are one of the oldest chicken breeds, described by Marco Polo as having hair like cats. They are about a third of the size of a chicken but look like a cross between a bird and a rabbit as their coat is more like fur or down than feathers. This down means that silkies are unable to fly, which is one reason I kept them in an ark, rather than letting them roam free range. They are also unusual in that they have five toes, black skin, plus a pompom head which covers their eyes and earlobes of a brilliant, turquoise blue. A hen the colour of a fresh conker was surprisingly warm when I picked her up, like a fluffy, breathing hot water bottle. I held her close and gently for a while, enjoying the living warmth.

Frost translates as *rhew* in Welsh, and one of our fields was called Parc Penrhew as it lay to the north and was always the last field to see the sun and the first to see it leave. We knew it as Frosty field. Old field names are fascinating in that they often just explain where a field is or what it does. I made my way downwards through Shed field to see the namescape. Sun cups littered the upper field, which had been able to capture and hold onto a few of the rays of the sun and I could see across to the opposite hills towards Monnington and Moylegrove, a patchwork of eiderdown fields, outlined and criss-crossed with the black running stitch of the hedge lines. Roll upon roll of clouds billowed over the hills, cotton white with a hint of apricot, and the sun was just beginning to beckon from the south. Wood pigeons startled out of an ash tree, wings clapping as if they were applauding the snowfall, and starlings scattered like wind tossed leaves thrown into the air. The sky started to brighten as I walked, the deep snow as difficult to walk in as sand, the northern sky a steel-blue, clouds outlined in aqua.

In spring, Penrhew field was covered in dandelions, so many you could hardly see any grass, just golden faces turning towards the sun before the puffball seed heads transformed the field into a place of wishes. According to folklore, dandelions are the star children of father sun and mother moon, which have fallen to earth and are unable to return, so the sun transforms them into star parachutes so they are able to fly home. The field could have been called dandelion field, or Parc Dant y llew.

Now they were hidden, as was everything. I walked a circuit alongside the hedgeline, my feet marking only a temporary path as true paths need to be continuously walked upon. The snow crunched, scintillas of different stars gleaming and glistening under my feet. Alongside, arrowheads of tracks ran in threads, in circles, in repeated lines all about, up, down, sideways through the field; the visible memories of footsteps of birds looking for food, all of us running around, searching for something lost.

~ *Nests* ~

'*...and most I like the winter nests*
deep hid
That leaves and berries fell into...'
(Edward Thomas)

February has always been my least favourite month. Even though it's the shortest – *y mis bach*, the little month – it seems to go on forever. As the last month of winter, it bridges the gap into spring, when we've had enough of gales and rain and mud and long for warmth and sun and the green of new life. By the time February comes, every leaf that didn't fall naturally in the autumn has been pulled from its home by the winter storms and now the only thing to be seen in the denuded branches are the remains of bird nests clinging tightly to their hosts.

Today is the first day of the month which is the beginning of the Celtic celebration of Imbolc, and the festival of Brigid, a goddess who brings light and life to the land. It's a rare, pale-sunshine day, a day when you start to believe that change is on its way. Walking across the fields, the ground underfoot isn't quite as claggy, the breeze blowing from the sea not so raw. Tree trunks and branches are black-soaked, the hedges a thickness of brown. But if you look closely enough, tiny buds of hawthorn are preparing to emerge, and an occasional hazel catkin, safe in the hollow of a protective arm of ash, trembles, naked in the cold.

Amongst the yards of hedges that enclose, bisect, protect and divide the fields, five apple trees are scattered amongst them. I'm not sure if they're wild apples or crab apples but prefer to think of them as the throw-away result of a farmer's lunch, maybe an apple he'd eaten along with some bread and cheese, or one a child ate whilst out playing.

There's a single apple tree growing near the cromlech in Rhiannon's field, disrupting the head-high hedge line. Thankfully, the farmers of before left it alone when they cut the hedge every autumn. The tree is old and has lost many branches and there's a dog-leg of a trunk that reaches into the field at just the right height for the sheep to scratch against. Silver and sage-green lichen smother its older branches, which are covered in a bridesmaid pink-and-white froth of blossom in May and by handfuls of rough, russet-green fruit in September. They are Haribo-sour to us, but the blackbirds and fieldfares seem to enjoy them. I make apple jelly from them every autumn, either blending them with sloes from the blackthorn growing at the feet of the apple tree to make a tart purple jelly that wobbles when you touch it and which is good to eat with cheese, or with the mint that grows like a weed amongst the roses and is good to eat with anything.

On top of this tree is a crow's nest, holding on with bony fingers. It's more like a collection of sticks rather than a well-designed home and is haphazard and large and too high for me to see the reported lining of moss and grass and anything else the crows find that softens and protects. A crow's nest takes two weeks to build and is home to the parents and their young for only nine. It is rarely re-used but can be added to over the following years if trees are sparse in the area. In spring, the ground underneath becomes littered with small branches and twigs. These are rejects – the crow is always selective in his choice of building material. He likes ones that are HB pencil-sized and will rarely fly down and select one he's discarded. A reject is always a reject.

The so-called crow's nest used as a lookout on the top of a ships mast may have originated from the Viking tradition of carrying crows on their long voyages, which they released in periods of poor visibility knowing the crow would fly towards land. Or it may just be that the small barrow-like contraption seen from the deck looked like a nest.

Crows are members of the Corvid family, which includes ravens, choughs and jays. They don't walk but strut, puffing their chests out like a cockerel. They have glistening stygian feathers, iridescent like the inside of a mussel shell when the light falls on them, and their beaks are long and pointed and curve down slightly at the end. They are intelligent beings and can remember people's faces, so you must treat them with respect – they can apparently relay their displeasure to other crows if you don't. There might be a reason why a group of crows is called a murder. If one of their flock dies, they mark the event by standing in a circle around their fallen companion as if in contemplation. Scientists believe they do this so they might learn more about why the bird has died rather than as a sign of distress. If you study a crow even for a short time, there is something otherworldly about them; they seem to be at the fringes of our world looking in. Max Porter's *Grief Is The Thing With Feathers*, and *Crow* by Ted Hughes, both use Crow as a metaphor for grief, death and life.

The crow becomes interchangeable with ravens in mythology, both being big, black birds, and are seen as birds of transformation, keepers of secrets, tricksters and also harbingers of death. When King Arthur was killed, his spirit supposedly passed into the chough, whose legs and beak turned red with his blood. The chough is a rare bird, found mainly on the western coastlines of Wales, Cornwall, Ireland and Brittany, interestingly the so-called Celtic nations. I've seen them and heard their distinctive call (which is a bit like a wheezy cough) in nearby Ceibwr and at Strumble head, further along the coast.

Last year, a young crow, dark-grey and tousled around the edges, became tangled in an old and twisted hawthorn, one foot caught on something out of sight. It kept still as I approached, which was unusual – most birds will sensibly try to fly away when a human approaches. Unwinding the cord which had become wrapped around the foot, the bird stared at a point above my head with forget-me-not blue eyes, and remained still, staring unblinkingly at the sky until it was safe to fly away. It was almost as if by not acknowledging me, I didn't exist. I hadn't realised that young crows have blue eyes, like human babies.

There are as many myths and legends associated with the apple tree as there are with crows. They are considered to be the oldest tree of all and represent immortality, their fruit being of the otherworld and of the gods. They symbolise the giving of love and are represented by the goddesses Venus and Olwen. According to legend, the apple orchards of paradise were known as the 'Isle of the blessed' and they housed the tree of knowledge upon which three sacred apple trees grew. The serpent that guarded the trees and the knowledge of the seasons was the goddess, Ceridwen. In the garden of Eden, the serpent became representative of the woman as a temptress, whilst the apple tree became the symbolic fruit of the downfall of man. The fairy-tale of Snow-White mirrors the story of the poisoned apple representing seduction, false knowledge, and wickedness.

The mythical island of Avalon, *Ynys Afallach*, in Welsh, means the Isle of Apples, and was ruled by the enchantress Morgan le Fey and is reputedly where King Arthur was taken to heal from his wounds. The wizard Merlin was believed to have worked in a grove of apple trees guarded by birds.

During the Welsh Cad Goddeu (the Battle of the trees), the apple was described as the 'most noblest tree of all'. Druids' wands were made from apple or yew and the fact that mistletoe often grows amongst its branches, made the apple a tree to be revered, mistletoe being another sacred plant. The star shaped core seen when you cut an apple in half meant it was seen as a natural pentagram and was often used in magical rituals.

Although an apple tree was seen as a symbol of plenty, felling one was considered to bring bad luck, and burning one sacrilegious. In Brehon law, it was one of their Chieftain trees, and the fine for felling one was three cows. The reason that lightning rarely splits apple trees is believed to be because it contains an abundance of love, and for both of these reasons, people planted apple trees near to their homes.

According to Dr Edward Bach, a homeopath and bacteriologist, who developed the use of flowers as natural remedies, the essence of apple is used for curing self-doubt, despondency, obsession, over-anxiousness and when getting stuck over details.

Perhaps these qualities influenced Newton which, after seeing an apple fall whilst he was sitting under an apple tree, led to his observations on the theory of gravity – the tree, a 'Flower of Kent' variety, still exists, protected by the National Trust in Lincolnshire.

The apple tree is a member of the Rose family, and all domestic apples are the same species, *Malus pumila*, which originated in Tien Shan, in north-western China. Bees can smell an apple in bloom from a third of a mile away, and in May, standing underneath the tree, I watch them working, and when close enough, see what colour their pollen bags are. Apple pollen is Tango-orange, brighter than the chestnut brown from the gorse, the darker brown of the red clover, the yellow brown of the wild cherry. The honey they make from the apple is light gold in colour and not too sweet and it carries just a tang of apple. Ninety-seven percent of all pollination in orchards is carried out by honeybees, so many commercial orchards keep bees as well.

In 1998, the so-called 'rarest apple tree in the world', *Afal Ynys Enlli*, was discovered not too far from here, on the windswept island of Bardsey in North Wales, and is supposedly the only remnant of a monastic orchard. It is also known as Merlin's apple as where it was found – opposite a mountainside with a cave – is reputedly where Merlin is buried in a glass coffin. Now available commercially, I have a small tree growing alongside an Annie Elizabeth, a Rosemary Russet and a Fiesta in Gwair field. Unlike the others, it hasn't borne any of its pink-streaked fruit yet. Maybe this year.

A thing of beauty, history, mythology and culinary use, how important are these trees today? How many of us see these things behind the blossom and the fruit? I'd like to think Crow did and chose this apple tree deliberately – they are clever birds, after all – but it was probably chosen because when perching high in their nest, they have a 360-degree birds-eye view over Rhiannon and Cromlech fields, the two fields lying either side of the hedge, and it's near enough for them to be able to raid the bird feeder when they felt like it.

One crow waits for me every morning as I fill them up. He's always in the same place and struts behind me as I add fat balls, which are his favourite. As soon as I leave, he'll race the magpie onto the feeder, swinging iridescently from side-to-side like an over-large trapeze artist – he's too heavy for it really. The guinea fowl try to rush him away, wings outstretched and alarm-calling, but he stands his ground, as do they.

In a distant life we walked alongside lions and elephants, they seem to say, you don't scare us…

But I am immortalised in stories and legends and walk with the gods, replies Crow…

If you walk further down the hedge line and follow it along the corner where it crosses Penrallt field, a nest the size of a Seville orange is half-hidden in a narrow tree near to the gate. It's the nest of a Goldfinch and nestles in the vee of the only cherry-plum tree on the farm, sitting at the level of the hedge-cutting three years ago which is just above eye height. The nest is cone shaped and made from thin stems, moss, grass and wool with a cup-centre that's as smooth as a puddled pond. This one has lichen around one edge, now flaking and dry, and although flowers are sometimes woven between the stems, there is no evidence of these now. The female builds the nest in about a week and lays around five eggs of a clotted-cream colour with milk-chocolate specks. She alone will incubate them, but the male will turn up to help feed the young once they've hatched. Goldfinch have slender bills adapted to eat seeds, although they will feed their young on insects such as aphids. Teasel and thistles are favourite foods although only the male can eat teasel seeds as his beak is slightly longer than the females. One of its local names is Thisteltuige, an Anglo-Saxon name meaning thistle-tweaker, other names being Redcap and King Harry.

Goldfinches are striking birds, with black and yellow wings, a buff-brown and cream body, a black head with white cheeks and a dipped-red face. Legend says that the goldfinch tried to remove the thorns from the crown placed on Jesus's head, the blood seeping into and permanently marking its face.

In Italian Renaissance painting, the goldfinch was used as a symbol of Christian redemption and there are almost 500 paintings featuring the bird including Raphael's *Madonna of the Goldfinch* which shows a young Christ reaching out to touch a goldfinch held by a young John the Baptist.

Its colouring and liquid-song call was the reason that many were trapped and kept as caged songbirds in Victorian times, and they could also be trained to carry-out simple tricks, such as lifting a thimble full of water. The decline in their numbers only halted when the Royal Society for the Protection of Birds intervened and the population began to increase.

Finding a goldfinch nest in this field was unexpected. Perhaps the long grass left around the edges of the field and now sprinkled with the remains of creeping thistle have persuaded them to spread further. In Autumn, they flock around the surrounding lane and the top fields near to the quarry where the ground is dry and the thistles, dock and orach run to seed more quickly. Since I've not cut the verges the last two years, there are more of these particular plants. Goldfinches are easy to identify with their vivid colouring and continuous peeping and twittering. They sometimes fly with linnets and redpolls, their yellow wing flashes blinking amongst the wave of red, gold and brown rippling through the long grasses.

The cherry plum in which the nest sits is a pretty tree in early spring. It's the first tree to flower, beating the blackthorn by a couple of weeks. In the Victorian language of flowers, the cherry-plum symbolises deception. The flowers are similar to blackthorn; five white petals with a froth of primrose-yellow stamens in their centre, delicate stars of white sprinkled against the dark. Whereas when the blackthorn comes into flower, the whole tree becomes submerged in an icing-sugar coating. A hedge line of blackthorn is a beautiful thing.

Cherry plums, or as they are sometimes known, Myrobalan plums, were often planted as a shelter belt for orchards – they have been traced back to the 1700s – and although they can grow up to 20 feet, when pruned, they make a good, dense hedge being fast growing and suitable for coastal and windy areas, such as here in Penrallt field, where the wind from the sea blows straight across the valley.

Cherry plum is used in Bach's flower remedies as a remedy for people in fear of losing control, including hurting others or themselves, or acting irrationally. Cherry plum essence can be used to give you the courage to follow your own path. It is one of the five flowers used for Dr Bach's Rescue remedy, a mix created to deal with immediate emergencies and crises, the others being star of Bethlehem, rock rose, impatiens and clematis. It is also recommended to take before exams. As a homeopathic practitioner, Dr Edward Bach travelled through Wales and the UK between 1930 and 1934 to research flowers he believed would provide a safe and natural method of healing.

This cherry plum is growing in my favourite hedge on the farm, favourite because there are many different varieties of plants entwined along it. Blackthorn and hawthorn are the two stalwarts and are both stunning in spring and autumn, especially now since nothing has been pruned for three years. There is also a spreading sycamore, goat willow, hazel, elder, a field maple (the only one on the farm and which turns a burning crimson, madder and butter-yellow in the autumn) and three wild cherry trees. These bear drifts of white flowers in April which appear before the leaves like blackthorn, and clusters of small yellow-red berries in August, not that you get to see a lot of them as the blackbirds enjoy eating them. I found a missed cluster once – the fruit is smaller and has a more bitter taste than the cultivated variety. The cherry tree bark is a rough, russet-brown with horizontal bands and can peel off in strips and the wood is considered useful for furniture making and turning. The first spoon I made was out of cherry wood, the colour resembling that of a freshly-hatched conker. In folklore, a cuckoo has to eat three good meals of cherries before it stops singing. They must have eaten bushels of fruit here, as I have never heard or seen one on the farm.

~ *A Suffragette Spring* ~

Today, Spring is the colour purple. Purple, white and green. From my limited viewpoint out of the kitchen window, ribbons of violet, lavender, mauve, lilac, indigo and white crocus wander between a sward of fresh green. Their flowers arch from a cluster of thin, straplike leaves, which have a chalk-line drawn down the centre of them. A finger-touch of sun is all that's needed for the tulip-shaped flowers to open like sea anemones, their golden stamens trembling in the March breeze. One has caught a fat bumblebee. It has a tawny, chenille bottom and climbs lazily over the petals with sherbet-dusted legs, as if just woken from a soporific slumber.

The carpet of amethyst starfish-like *Crocus tommasinianus* that hide under the cherry tree have been replaced by their more voluptuous cousins which prefer to exhibit themselves under a full sun. 'Ruby Giant' spreads indiscriminately. Its name is somewhat misleading, as it is neither red nor large. It stands four inches tall, and its colour is a rich, deep violet, fading gently towards its egg-yolk centre. Originally from southern Europe, it was introduced to Britain in 1936. It drifts amongst the paler colour of *Crocus chrysanthus* 'Blue Pearl'. Their goblet shaped flowers aren't blue, but a beautiful, iridescent, washed lavender, with tiny purple brushstrokes pointing towards the stem. The petals have a silvery sheen and gleam in the early spring light. It has a faint, sweet perfume, although you have to lie down to appreciate it. Not as prolific as the above, another snow crocus is the elegant 'Snow Bunting'. It's a pure, gleaming, bright white with a smudge-of-smoke feathering on its outer petals, a throat of butter-yellow, and it too has a delicate scent. 'Snow

Bunting', was introduced here in 1914 and was named after the bird Plectrophenax nivalis, which breeds in places such as Iceland, Greenland and the mountains of Scotland. This white winged sparrow-like bird flies down to the sea from its breeding ground in the mountains during November to February, the same time the crocus is in flower. Here, the blooms burst open amongst the dark green, flat, matt leaves of the soon-to-be-open daisies and the newness of the grass, which needs a temperature of over six degrees to initiate growth, knitted with the asparagus-spears of daffodil leaves.

The name Crocus originated from the Greek, 'Krokos' meaning saffron, although the species that produce the most expensive spice in the world flower in the autumn, and are a rich, golden yellow. It can take 75,000 flowers to produce one pound of the spice.

Spring flowering crocus thrive on a rocky soil in thin grassland, and their leaves die down entirely after flowering. In Greek mythology, Crocus was a noble youth, who killed himself when he was forbidden to marry the girl he loved. Knowing this, it's strange that in the language of flowers, the crocus stands for cheerfulness and new beginnings. In America, it's often known as the 'light bulb' flower as it brightens up the world after the darkness of winter.

Purple, green and white – the colours representing the suffragette movement in England. Dress and attire became an important part of their campaign. In 1908, Emmeline Pethick-Lawrence, co-editor of the *Votes for Women* magazine, and member of the Woman's Social and Political Union (WSPU) wrote 'Be guided by the colours in your choice of dress…we have seven hundred banners in purple, white and green.'

The colours had been chosen symbolically. Purple stood for loyalty, freedom and dignity, white for purity and green for hope, and if you replace the purple with violet, the initials of Green, White, Violet, stand for Give Women Votes. Members were encouraged to wear these colours as 'a duty and a privilege' and to dress smartly and fashionably to detract from their negative stereotypical image drawn by the cartoonists of the day. Sylvia Pankhurst, a founder member of the WSPU, designed many of the items worn, and members often chose jewellery to correspond with the colours, the semi-precious stones used including amethyst, pearls and peridot. This 'branding', now common today, was one of the first of its kind to promote a movement, the colours becoming instantly recognisable as those of the suffragettes.

In America, gold replaced green, the colour representing the colour of light and life. In 1867, the Kansas suffragists adopted the state flower, the sunflower, as a symbol of their campaign, '…the torch that guides our purpose, pure and unswerving.' They lost their battle to win the vote at that time, but the colour gold was adopted by the national movement. Gold pins, sashes and yellow roses become recognisable symbols of their cause.

Maine suffragists chose the daffodil as their symbolic flower. This smaller flower was easier to carry or wear and could be 'forced' to bloom earlier or later, so could be picked for a longer time.

Further up the lane, where the grass becomes wiry and tough, the first of the daffodils are piercing their way through the early spring soil. These are Tenby daffodils, reputed to be the original St. David's Day daffodil. Matt, glaucous and squat, which helps them withstand the wind that blows across from the sea or down from the Preseli mountains, they have cups and petals of the same shade of bright gold.

In my overgrown border, other varieties I've planted will soon start to make an appearance. Not for me, the blowsy, heavy-headed, frilled giants that abound in suburban gardens, the ones that snap with the hint of a puff of wind. I love the old, historic dancing varieties, ones that have stories to tell or have names that sing. My favourite is 'Bath's flame', which was introduced before the first world war and is the colour of a freshly cut pineapple, the petticoat of the cup dipped in burnt copper-red. Its head dips slightly and the elongated petals have a slight twist. It sways and bends with the breeze, as does its neighbour, 'White Lady', an even older variety, and popular as a cut flower between the wars. She has an elegant, drooping neck, and tissue paper-fine petals of white, which tilt as if shielding her face from the sun, her sherbet-lemon drop centre carrying a faint scent of hyacinth and vanilla.

The oldest of the bulbs, and one seen naturalised in many gardens nearby is the unusual Van Sion daffodil, or *Telamonius Plenus*. It has a double trumpet cup but can morph into a mop head, similar to the mane of a lion, reverting back the year after if it feels it wants to. The colour and shagginess alters according to the weather – if it's cold, the canary-bright yellow of the flower becomes streaked and splashed with lime-green. It's a strong grower here and naturalises easily. It was first reported flowering in the garden of a Vincent Sion in London, in 1620, and by the 1700s had spread to America, taken by British immigrants who settled in Kentucky, Tennessee and Virginia. Apparently, you can still find the plants in the original gardens of long-gone houses. Van Sion was also a favourite of the Native Americans who were forced to travel along the so-called 'Trail of Tears' to Oklahoma. And once freed, African American slaves transported the bulbs northwards to Mississippi and beyond, the Appalachian hills becoming covered with gold and green trumpets.

~ *A Place of Loss* ~

Dave loved Penbanc. He loved it almost as much as he loved his homeplace of East Sussex, whose deep clay and chalk downlands ran through him like letters in a stick of pink, peppermint rock. Sussex had become busy and expensive and we moved so he could follow his dream of owning his own land. His grandparents and great-grandparents had spent their lives farming, and that urge, the longing for that way of life, had always been with him. He loved the space here, the freedom of having his own farm and lands to do with as he wanted. He loved the names of the fields, even though he had less idea than I how to pronounce them and even less idea of what they meant. Parc Rhewllyd, Dai Llan, Cwm Isaf. Cromlech field was self-explanatory, even though a previous farmer had moved the stone to another field, Parc y shed, (I apologise to it every time I walk past), a field I re-named Rhiannon. We had an Arthur's seat in one of the lower fields, so I felt we could do with some more female energy.

   A small stream runs at the bottom of the fields, gentle in the summer and raging in the winter. It becomes Nant Ceibwr further down the valley and flows through the villages of Monington and Moylegrove before joining the sea at Ceibwr Bay, another name that has various pronunciations depending on which farm you come from. Having spent many hours at Poohstick bridge in the Ashdown Forest when the children were young, following the tradition of dropping twigs over one side of the bridge and rushing to the other side to see whose came first, we often talked about one of us waiting at the bay whilst the other dropped something in the water at home, just to see how long it would take for it to travel to the sea.

The farmers of Tregamman, Hafod Grove, Blaenawen and Trefaes Ganol took Dave to their taciturn hearts. He would turn up on their doorsteps asking for advice, or just to see if he could have a look around. Within months, they would reciprocate, ending up drinking tea in our kitchen, talking of all things sheep and farms. Badgers were a common and interesting point of discussion, as was the EU and rugby. The neighbours even gave him a 'Welsh' name, Dai Twndish, *twndish* being Welsh for a funnel, thus making him an honorary Welshman in their eyes, which was something he was proud of – apart from when the rugby was on. Then he was English through and through.

Dave was so happy living in Penbanc, he never wanted to go on holiday.

'Why would I want to go away?' he used to say, 'I've got everything I ever wanted here.'

Needless to say, we did get away. I didn't share his opinion. There were too many places in the world that I wanted to see, so I picked my moment to discuss the subject with him after he'd had a few beers. We happened to be away on holiday with friends in France when he became ill. The pressure in the aeroplane on the flight causing the tumour that had been insidiously growing inside his head to swell considerably, resulting in weakness in his legs and an ever-increasing headache.

'I told you we should never go away,' he said, only half-jokingly, when he was admitted to the hospital in Nimes.

Glioblastoma multiforme, or GBM to those in the know is, by definition, a grade 4, terminal brain tumour. It is the king of all tumours, or more like a king with an invading army, slashing and burning as they go. A GBM4 is exceedingly fast growing, with tendrils that spread out from the main bulk, like the stinging, sucking tentacles of a squid, or a man-o-war, so even if the surgeons manage to remove the body of the tumour, it's likely to have spread throughout the brain already. There is no cure. Treatment is palliative and aimed at minimising symptoms, the gold standard being surgery, to remove as much of the tumour as possible, followed by radiotherapy, then chemotherapy. The average age of diagnosis is 55, men being affected more than women, and tall men even more so. Dave was 54 and 6 foot three inches tall. The time between diagnosis to death is three months without treatment, and 12-15 months with. He died almost exactly a year after diagnosis.

Our life changed overnight. He had to sell his beloved sheep, lost his driving licence, lost his gun licence and gradually, inexorably, lost himself.

One thing about a terminal prognosis, rather than a sudden death, is that you can plan what you'd like to happen to you regarding how and where you die, and what you want as far as a funeral was concerned. Whether or not that's a good thing, I'm undecided. We talked about his funeral. We discussed coffins. Who knew there were so many? Coffins made from oak, mahogany, pine, wicker, cardboard, bamboo, seagrass. I found someone that made them from wool, which seemed appropriate, having something that reminded him of his sheep. He asked that I put a shank of sheep's wool in with him, an old shepherding tradition. Because shepherds had to watch their flock every day, they were unable to go to church on the sabbath. By putting wool in the coffin, come judgement day, you'd be forgiven, as God would know you were a shepherd. When the time came, I did this for him, cutting a curl from one of my pet sheep, placing it on top of his chest alongside his favourite beer glass, his sheepdog whistle and a photograph of all of us, so he couldn't forget us, even if he wanted to.

John, the gently spoken vicar from Nevern church came around a few times to discuss arrangements, and to talk to Dave. He was a kind, compassionate man, who'd lost his wife the year before. Dave had been brought up as a Strict Baptist but left the church as soon as he could. The Strict Baptist message was definitely a strict one; women not being allowed to speak in church being only one aspect that he didn't agree with. He did like to talk about religion though, even though he had no such beliefs himself. He would willingly ask the Jehovah's Witnesses to come in and talk over a cup of tea, so he could have a discussion with them. They visited many times and were so kind after he was diagnosed.

As the disease marched onward, his religious views began to change. I don't know whether it was because he knew he was dying and things take on a different significance when you're close to leaving your life, or whether the advancing tumour was affecting the part of his brain responsible for those feelings. This part of his behaviour was so different to what 'our' Dave had been like, but it gave him comfort, and there was little of that around.

Grief bogged us down and affected everything we did. There was a miasma of it clogging up the house and the land. Grief became mixed in with feelings of guilt. I'd always worked with sick people, my area of specialism being neurology – head injuries, stroke, Parkinson's disease, but now my husband was dying of something in his brain, and I couldn't do a thing about it. The only thing I could do was to support him in his wish to die at home.

He began to resemble one of the fallen oak trees brought down in the storms. He'd always been so strong, so able. He'd played second row in the scrum; would build fence posts by hand rather than use a tractor; chopped wood; laid hedges; sheared sheep; built me a deck amongst the trees. Over a couple of months, his leg muscles resembled branches rather than trunks, and the steroids he had to take made him look like an angry puffer fish, even when his vast appetite faded to nothing. He hated it.

The weather was glorious on the day he died. I had a feeling he would leave us on that particular day, one week after our wedding anniversary. He'd managed to stay alive for our daughter's wedding three weeks previously, and he'd had enough. He lay in the loaned hospital bed downstairs in the front room, whilst we sat just outside his window so he could hear us talking and I opened every door and window in the house to let the warmth and the sunshine and the smell of honeysuckle in, and to let what was left of him fly out alongside the buzzards and red kites he loved so much.

As we'd talked about his funeral a number of times, I knew what he wanted. I'd chosen '*Fields of Gold*' by Sting, for him to come into the church – I wanted something to remind him, and us, of his fields. We sang his favourite hymns, '*The day thou gavest…*' and '*Cwm Rhondda*', the same tunes we had sung for my dad's funeral six months before. He'd loved to hear what he called 'proper' singing, so I found a Welsh male soloist to sing '*Swing Low, Sweet Chariot*' as a nod to his love of rugby. The singer sang it beautifully, without accompaniment, although I did notice the staunch Welsh contingent wincing a little. A dear friend did a reading that Dave had heard on the radio a few weeks previously, and I wrote an elegy that I managed to say without crying. I felt numb actually. He'd requested '*A Wonderful World*' by Louis Armstrong to leave by. He still thought it was.

He'd wanted to leave from the farm, so he did. We took our last journey together past his barns, his fields, his dogs and the remaining animals. I'd asked the florist to cover the top of the coffin in wild and country-garden flowers: daisies, cornflowers, sweet William, larkspur, snapdragon, poppy seed heads, lady's mantle, corn, so it resembled a meadow, and we decorated his shepherd's crook with the same. A friend of his, John, owned a Harley Davidson dealership in Sussex, and a few months before his death, Dave decided that he would quite like a motorbike send-off. John was very keen to do anything to help, so a motorbike send-off he had: four very noisy, huge Harleys disrupting the quiet journey to the church. I think the neighbours were slightly bemused; I'm sure they would have been happy to have given him a tractor send-off if he'd asked.

Everyone came back to the farm afterwards. Dave had loved a party, so that's what we had. We cleaned up the Dutch barn and put the food and drink in there. His favourite food was curry and burgers, so we made the first and hired a burger-and-hot-dog van for the second. The neighbours made Welsh cakes and numerous variations of Bara Brith, and my mum was in her element making tea, so she could find out who everyone was, where they lived and what they did for a living.

We had a bar in the barn as well, and everyone did their best to drink it dry. Dave had loved beer and cocktails – he'd enjoyed making them – so we had those too. His favourite had been a Long Island Iced Tea, which is made from five clear spirits and a dash of coke, so it resembles tea. They look innocuous but they are not.

The party carried on until the early hours, and the darkening night became full of Eighties music and 'do you remembers' and 'I wish's'. People took it in turns to drive his quad bike around the field, and I quashed my normal thoughts of helmets and head injuries. A friend left saying, 'That was the best funeral I've ever been to. Dai would have loved it.'

And if he'd been there, he would have done.

A year and a half later, I had a telephone call from the stonemason, saying that the headstone for Dave's grave was ready. At last. One of the reasons I'd chosen this particular company was because of its name – *Grave Concerns* – which made me smile. As little else did, I reasoned it was a good choice. I'd wanted the outline of an oak tree on the stone, so it had to be sent away to be engraved.

'There's a bit of a problem,' he said.

'What sort of a problem?'

'Well…they've spelt his name wrong.'

'How can you miss-spell David!?'

'No, not David, the Welsh one.'

He meant Twndish. I'd wanted that written on there as well.

'But you're Welsh, and I checked the spelling with every Welsh speaker I know.'

'I know, but they obviously didn't agree.'
'Where did you send it? England?'
'No, North Wales.'

So, his Welsh name on his gravestone is spelt wrongly, Twn dish, not Twndish. We talked about getting a new stone, but decided that Dave would see the funny side, so we left it as it was.

~ *An Oak and a Kite* ~

It's the first day of spring and the oak tree at the end of the track is starting to show signs of new life. The ivy that pulled its way up through the branches has remained a forest-green all winter, so the oak never looks bare, even though the winter wind blew away the last of the bleached marcesence of leaves that had been stubbornly clinging to its lower branches. The new leaves are a subtle, smooth shininess of copper-brown, which will evolve through mustard and a fizz of lime to a bright green in a few months. They will merge and blend with the canopy of ash, sycamore and hornbeam that help protect the lower growing hazel and birch and by high summer it will be difficult to tell where one tree ends and another begins.

It is said that the so-called 'King of the Forest' spends 300 years growing, 300 years resting and 300 years dying. Each tree is a habitat in itself, supporting hundreds of species of wildlife, including the woodpecker, treecreeper, long-tailed tit, jay and squirrel. According to mythology, tree nymphs called hamadryads inhabit oak trees and were companions to Artemis, the Greek goddess of hunting. The druids believed the energy, power and strength of their god, Esus, were represented in the oak, and Herne the hunter and Gwyn-Ap-Nudd, the ruler of the Welsh otherworld, Annwn – whose hounds hunt souls across the sky – inhabit oak forests. Oak was one of the nine flowers that were used to create the goddess Blodeuwedd, whose name is also the ancient name for the owl in which she was turned into.

The oaks in this wood are Sessile oaks, not English. Sessile oaks are squat and broad, and their branches are twisted and gnarled. They are the trees of fairy tales and legends, dreams and nightmares. The bark of the tree is furrowed, wet-concrete grey, with a continuum of cracks, so rainwater can be funnelled to the ground from the top of the tree. It is rough and tough and cool to touch. Tannin in oaks was once used to tan leather, and its heavy, dense timber used for making furniture, building houses and ships. Jason's ship the *Argo* was constructed from a sacred oak, as was King Arthur's round table.

The usefulness of this tree is probably one of the reasons why there are few oaks left in this wood or nearby. Some have self-seeded in the sharp banks that edge their way to the stream and because there isn't enough soil to support them when they get to a certain height, a few have fallen and have just been left – no machine here can get close enough to pull them out. Some have grown wide and twisted, the eddies and scurries of wind creating fantastical shapes. They are covered with moss and silver-green lichen, ferns waterfalling from their upper branches. Further down the valley, one lies with half of its roots in the air. These are slowly strangling a marbled, quartz boulder, now at head-height, whilst the trunk has split into three, all growing. It resembles a washed-up sea creature from another time and place.

The oak at the bottom of the track is special. It's not the tallest, the widest or the most symmetrical, in fact it's quite uneven since a large bough snapped like a twiglet two winters ago, and the gap it left hasn't been filled yet. The reason it's special is because, until last year, red kites nested there.

Brought back from near extinction, they are a common sight here, especially during lambing when there is a plentiful supply of food, and when the farmers are making hay or silage. They cruise the airways, tails a-tilt, alongside screaming gulls and crows, waiting to see what the fields have to offer. They are opportunistic feeders, preferring carrion to live prey, although they reputedly kill small birds and mammals if nothing else is available. They will eat early-morning earthworms, although I've only seen buzzards do this. Kites have always struck me as inherently indolent birds, maybe because they soar slowly rather than flap, propelling themselves through the air with minimal effort, one deep wingbeat enabling them to travel the length of the field. They appear almost weightless, gliding and banking, changing direction without effort just by a flick of their tail. Maybe because they only weigh about a kilo, which seems insubstantial for their size. They are often mobbed by corvids but rise above it with grace and disdain. They are noble, aristocratic creatures, which fill me with delight whenever I see them.

Unlike their sleek beauty, their nest is a mess. A collection of sticks-and-moss mess, added to every year. They also pick up anything they think might add to the general untidiness – pieces of plastic, baler twine (bright-blue, in this nest), a sock that dropped from the washing line. Wool left over from last year's shearing has been used to soften this haphazardness, which is exaggerated when the adults start to feed their young – parts of a foraged lamb's coat dangling like a bizarre out-of-season Christmas decoration.

A smell of decay permeates the woodland at peak feeding time, stronger when you walk beneath the oak. This was especially noticeable one year when three young fledged and the adult birds seemed on a never-ending journey to provide food for their raucous brood. They became used to me walking under the tree every day and it was a privilege to see the young birds start to leave their nest. They would clumsily jump from branch to branch, spreading their wings experimentally, the closeness of the trees making it difficult for them to navigate a pathway. They screeched and hollered, still wanting food from their exhausted parents, leaping and hopping and flapping. Even though I knew they were big birds – their wingspan is at least the size of me – I hadn't appreciated how big they were until I was able to be so close to them. Five red kites in close proximity made me and this woodland seem small.

Their colouring is quite beautiful and distinct – a fox-red body feathering to blackened wing tips, with white patches when seen from underneath and a frosted-silver head streaked with ink. Their eyes, feet and hooked beak are all yellow, the beak seemingly small compared to the size of the bird.

    Within five days they were gone. The wood seemed quiet after the excitement. You were once again able to hear the blackbird, the wren, the woodpigeon. The oak stretched its branches around the empty nest and leaves snuck into the once-full corners. The lambswool stretched lower and lower after the rain and became streaked with green rather than rust-brown. In the autumn, I found fragments of bone, and bizarrely, a lamb's tail complete with an orange docking ring. Occasionally, a kite glided overhead and tilted its wings, just as a pilot would do as a gesture.

~ *Magazines.Shields.Headliner* ~
(What3words)

*(What3words
– encodes geographic coordinates
into three dictionary words)*

Many people don't notice the gentle hillock as they head towards the beaches at Newport or the shops and cafés in Cardigan town. It's along the road you traverse if you turn right at the end of our lane, the road that leads to Nevern where Dave is buried. There's only a two-car layby and a small plastic plaque that you'd have to stop to read, describing what's behind the stunted gorse and hawthorn hedge. But if you were to leave your car and walk about 250 steps, the view would be worth the effort.

On a clear day, there is a 360-degree view from the top of Crugai Cemmaes. The bronze age burial chamber lies camouflaged by untidy mounds of gorse, tussocks of rye grass and ever-increasing blackberry wands, that snake around your ankle when you're not looking. The gorse is just coming into flower – splashes of canary yellow against the greyness of grass after snow – whilst unfurled, crisp fronds of dead bracken underpin its windward side. The pale January sun is not yet strong enough to make it let go of its coconut scent. Sheep graze the lower slopes on the northern side, and in the spring, black-and-white cattle cavort on the lusher pasture to the south. Last summer, they broke free from the inadequate fencing and roamed over the mound before being re-captured, leaving steaming piles of manure and a legacy of wellington-boot deep ruts, which mud-sucked and soaked your feet in the winter, and over which you twisted your ankle in the summer.

Today it is Sunday-quiet at the summit – no distant hum of traffic or rattle of a tractor – only the sound of the easterly wind that buffets around this small outcrop, the coldness of it making my cheeks smart and my eyes water. It carries with it a hint of snow and the faint, sickly smell of slurry from a nearby field. A flock of small brown birds, linnet or redpoll, startle out of the twisted hedge, scattering like leaves blown by an October wind, and slate-headed fieldfare rattle-call as they search for the last of the autumn berries, ignoring the few remaining withered sloes that cling to the blackthorn. Few creatures can tolerate their bitterness, even in these lean winter months.

I lean against the stone marker, resting my elbows on the top. The cold roughness of the stone will eventually seep through my jacket, but until then, I'll gaze at the view. Fields with borders of brown and black fan below me, and an isolated plantation of conifers stand out in their dark racing greenness against the winter-faded colours. Beyond the fields, the pewter arc of Cardigan Bay stretches eastwards and to the west, the white bulk of one of the Irish Ferries fleet dwarfs Fishguard harbour.

To my left, the ancient volcano of Carn Ingli, or Mynydd Carn-Ingli, the Hill of angels, pierces the skyline. The summit features an iron age hillfort, one of the largest in West Wales, whilst the lower slopes show evidence of a bronze age settlement. St Brynach, who sailed to Wales from Ireland, reputably spoke with angels on its summit, before founding his church in nearby Nevern, where the yew tree bleeds and where Dave was laid to rest. When the top of the mountain is covered by ice-white streamers of cirrus cloud, the local people say that angels are flying over Carn Ingli. Apparently, sleeping on the summit makes you become a poet, turns you mad, or the angels will come and speak to you whilst you sleep. I'd be happy with the first or third, but maybe not the second.

With my back to the sea, the grey, craggy ridge of the Preseli mountains fills the sky, the slopes beneath lying copper-pink with heather and moss. An ancient super-highway, The Golden Road, dating back to 3000 BC, runs along its spine; supposedly called because gold mined in the Wicklow mountains in Ireland was carried along this route as far as Wessex. Bedd Arthur, high on the Preseli ridge and near to Carn

Bica, is reputedly one of the places where King Arthur was buried, whilst the bodies of several of his knights that were killed and turned to stone by Twrch Trwyth, an enchanted boar, lie near Cerrig Marchogion, the so-called rocks of the knights. Thirteen stones, plus two that have fallen, lie in an oval horseshoe, a similar pattern to the inner circle at Stonehenge. Bluestone slabs were quarried from these jagged, inhospitable peaks and transported to Stonehenge around 2900 BC, but some believe that some of the unspotted stones may originally have been part of a circle first created at Maun Wawn, in the peatland surrounding the Preseli's, then moved to Stonehenge. How incredible that 42 five-ton stones were transported from this windswept, magical landscape to a place 180 miles away. And that such a special place can be summed up in three words, or at least located by them. Magazines.Shields.Headliner

~ *A Drift of Rock and Sea* ~

The sea is creeping its way up the shoreline as I make my way across the slabs of slate that bridge Nant Ceibwr, the stream that gently empties into the sea at Ceibwr Bay on the North Pembrokeshire coast. To me, the word bay is something of a misnomer as the word sums up images of a wide, sweeping curve of sand and sea – Ceibwr is its pocket-size cousin.

It's warm for this time of year and the offshore wind does nothing more than lightly stir the hair at the nape of my neck. No clouds pierce the spring-blue translucency of the sky, against which the sea is a darker reflected labradorescence of turquoise, teal and aqua. The ruffle-lace tops of waves sigh as they touch and explore the shore … then a suck as the water is pulled backwards towards Ireland. It's a remote, rocky, wild place, with little parking for summer visitors. Two shouldering arms of cliffs enclose the inlet, formed where the earth's layers were thrown, moulded, twisted, and corrugated, the eroded fragments of which litter the shoreline – sandstone, mudstone and boulder clay. The landward side is marginally softened by Berber-tough grass, knotted with threads of yellow celandines, pink sea thrift and linen-white stitchwort, which, according to folklore, should never be picked in case it evokes thunder.

I crunch my way to the large boulders that are embedded in the right side of the beach. They are elephant-grey, fissured and cracked in some places and smooth and rounded in others, a combination of the earth's fury and the sea's never-ceasing attrition. The rock I sit on – angled and cold – lies in front of the chiaroscuro of caves. It's a microcosm of the landscape around me: moulded, striated, pewter-grey, with bladder-wrack clinging on with bulbous brown fingertips as the sun drains it of moisture, and a tide line of lettuce green moss, which springs back as I touch it, white-crusted with salt. An indentation at its foot cups a small pool of iced water.

A wren tic-tacs from the cappuccino froth of blackthorn above the cliff edge, the sound piercingly loud for such a diminutive bird, a chiffchaff chiff-chaffs, a cock blackbird trills a warning call, an escaped pheasant alarms, and a blackcap sings incessantly, a note-jumping warble like a scratchy 78 record on repeat.

A herring gull comes to join me, standing pink-ankled deep in the water, his head cocked, and he stares at me with primrose-cool eyes as if waiting for something. He's a handsome bird, with a cement-grey back and white chest, and a blood-red fingerprint on his beak. In a crowd, he'd be raucous, quarrelsome and noisy, but by himself, he has no need to be. He ducks under the waves several times, water droplets sheening off his head, and is eventually rewarded by the catch of a wriggling, sludge-brown crab. He takes an inordinately long time to eat it, stabbing and tearing and gulping. I've seen gulls gouge eyes from sheep, and I know what those vicious, golden beaks can do. When finished, he struts to the fresh water of Nant Ceibwr, drinking just where it merges with the salt. A male mallard watches from upstream, his peacock head iridescent in the sun and nearby a grey wagtail dips and flicks and darts.

In the vee between the headlands, five gannets cruise past, bone-white wings like sails, the tips dipped in ink. They move slowly, conserving energy for their arrowhead dives. Gannets often mean dolphins, but not today – there's no triangular darkness or crest of silver breaking the water.

A kestrel throws himself off the vertiginous cliff and I follow his gingerbread back and slate-blue head as he hovers and glides, hovers and glides, hovers and dives…

The longer I sit, the more I notice: a tiny stream of Evian-clear mountain water trickling down the side of the cliff and a rock pipit drinking from it, gripping onto the darkness of moss alongside; the dull sparkle and glisten of quartz crystal running through rocks as the sun hits them; a winking shard of aquamarine sea-glass, or mermaids' tears, as I prefer to call them, wedged between two stones; the undercurrent of drying seaweed lingering in the air.

Someone walks along the shore towards the caves, his scarlet shirt strident against the blue.
   He stops next to me, commenting on my paper and pad.
   'Are you drawing or writing?' he asks.
   'Writing.' I tell him what I'm writing about, and he tells me he's an artist. He paints with his partner; fantasy, otherworld, mixed-media creations, and is thinking about writing stories to go with his worlds. We discuss the colours of the sea, and he, with his artist's eye, joins my now external thoughts on how many words there are to describe it and the vastness of the sky. He comments on the orange-iron drip on the rocks opposite, which he thinks looks as if the rock had cried into the sea for aeons and I tell him that sometimes I think that the sea is full of the world's tears. He says that in his pictures, he draws doorways that lead into different worlds. A bit like Narnia? I ask. Yes, he replies, but with doors leading into more doors and more worlds. Well, if you want doorways and worlds within worlds, you need to walk a mile down the coast path to see the Witches' Cauldron, a sea cavern you can only reach by swimming, I say. The locals call it Ceridwen's cauldron, after the story in the Mabinogion, and who knows what sort of doorways you might find there…

The wind is stronger as I walk back up the path. The wagtail is still flitting amongst the fast-flowing water, stopping on occasional stones, and I startle a skylark, perched unusually statue-like on a fence. His crown feathers spring up in alarm, and he flies upwards almost vertically, like a tiny parachute going the wrong way. The air echoes with his call, but I soon lose sight of him. I'll walk to the Witches' Cauldron soon, I decide, to see what doorways I can find.

~ *The Witches' Cauldron* ~

Nature has moved on by the time I walk westwards along the coastal path to Pwll y Wrach, the Witches' Cauldron. It takes about twenty minutes without stopping, but longer if you want to admire the view (which of course you must) – the path is narrow and drops vertically towards the sea in places so it's not a good idea to walk and look at the same time. Near the shoreline, the sea is the colour of watered-down mud with swirls of olive and sage, and below the horizon, the offing swells with turquoise, teal and kingfisher blue. The wind is blowing straight off the sea, the sound bringing back a childhood memory of holding a shell up to my ear, and there's a distant boom echoing from a sea cave. Behind me, desiccated grasses whisper.

The path is lined with mounds of sea thrift, whose drumstick heads brush crisp against my leg, tiny pincushions of soft blue-mauve sheep bit, the low growing downy leaves of silverweed, velvety to touch, and clumps of sea campion, their flowers poking above their pink veined, balloon-like necks. Their leaves are a waxy emerald, and up close, the chalk white petals are dissected vertically, so it looks like a fine kohl pencil line has been drawn along them. Further along are small outcrops of gorse, topiarised by the wind, and as I stop behind them, I see three gannets heading westwards. One banks and turns and flies back the way he's come, ascends quickly then executes a perfect swallow dive. He surfaces empty-beaked and after a moment, takes flight again to continue on his way.

Turning a corner, past the stacks and buttresses of iron-grey rock thrusting skywards from a rolling sea, a male kestrel bursts out of the undergrowth. He hovers at eye height – the advantage of walking along a cliff path. He's so close, I can see the trembling of his wings and the tilt of his tail, which spreads like a perfect art deco fan, his head remaining perfectly still as he focuses.

I leave him to his deadly contemplation and continue walking. The wind drops a little as I turn the corner, and in a nook created by a stunted blackthorn, a tiny blue butterfly nestles down – a common blue, I think – and a bee clings to a candy pink-and-white trumpet bloom of a field bindweed that winds widdershins through the scrub. Below the path, I spot the brown back of the female kestrel skimming the cliff edge. I follow her for a while before she disappears into one of the deep fissures that bisect the rocky outcrop.

Far below I see a slow-moving patch of a different colour from the sea. It hugs the shoreline, bobbing gently with the waves, and I stop to try and see what it is. We saw a sunfish here a few years ago, which I originally thought was a jellyfish brought inland by the wind, or a seal hovering just below the surface, but then spotted a fin and a paler, large oblong body as it steered lazily around the headland. However, today's sighting wasn't a sunfish. Smaller and tide-driven, it was a plastic bag, half full of air, clogging the sea.

It's a steep slope down towards the cauldron and I slip on the scattering of pebbles covering the dry rock, disturbing a flock of small brown birds crowding the path and a crow which startles seawards out of the heather. I look to see if it has the distinctive red legs and red beak of a chough, but unfortunately not.

The cauldron is a collapsed sea cave. A stream disappears into it on one side and on the other, a passage connects it to the sea. There's been a recent rock-fall, the evidence pouring onto the small shingle beach, which is only accessible by water. The sides are angled steep, and, on the right, there are patches of green, scattered with white flowers. Two pigeons don't seem to mind the drop, as they sit and coo. The cliff path forms a bridge over the water from which you can see the waves surging through the gap that leads into the cauldron. It boils and mists, trying to force its way in, but becomes limpid and silvery-smooth once inside. In the network of the caves that bisect and cross far beneath my feet, the colour of the water is apparently a bright emerald green, especially in the inaccessible chinks and crevices into which the kayaks cannot reach. It feels strange that so much is happening underneath me, a subterranean world that only things of the sea and the earth can see, and I feel the sense of a magical, otherworld place. The reported sighting of a mermaid in 1860 seems believable to me, especially on this day of wind and spray and bursts of sun and with no other person in sight.

Legend says that the cavern is the lair of a sea witch who would eat anyone who was foolish or brave enough to venture into her kingdom. Years later, people would come to consult this reputed witch, and maybe this, and the presence of an iron-rich spring called Ffynnon Alwm and an iron-age fort called Castell Tre-Riffith nearby, is why the area became known as Ceridwen's cauldron; caverns and springs and castles being things that myths are made of.

I turn back the way I've come, which is a steep climb upwards. Two birds fly out of the gorse and one tightropes on a narrow stem, gently bouncing up and down. For a moment I can see it clearly – its long-angled tail and red eyes give it away. They're Dartford warblers, such pretty birds with slate-grey pompom heads, a rust-red breast and matching eye stripes. I haven't seen one in years and the sight of them makes the climb worthwhile.

They take flight high above the cliff where the blue-wash of sky is tumbled by great mounds of clouds, their outlines backlit by an invisible sun, whilst out to sea, white horsetails flick their way northwards across Cardigan Bay.

~ 'Gog and Magog' ~

*Trees are the guardian spirits of the
land, therefore angels.*

(Roger Deakin)

The oak tree fell down in January, pole-axed by a rare blast of northerly wind. The usual wind direction here is a wet and windy westerly – when the north wind blows, we rarely have snow, just fallen branches or trees. Because of the way the land lies, the wind funnels up from the lower cwm, races upwards through the steep sides of the small valley lined with trees, and bursts into the widening woodland, forming miniature vortexes that batter anything that gets in their way. And this time, Magog had been caught in the maelstrom.

Gog and Magog. A pair of sessile oaks I'd named after the two ancient oaks of Avalon who'd heralded the entrance onto the isle. They were part of a druidic avenue leading towards Glastonbury Tor and were themselves named after two biblical apocalyptical figures. Reputedly 2000 years old, Magog is now reaching the end of her natural life and unfortunately the original Gog recently died following a fire.

The air is still today, full of the hush that often follows bad weather. It's almost as if the earth is taking a breath to recover from the chaos of the day before. Wisps of cloud, lace-white against the fresh blueness of the sky, travel slowly eastwards and drips of sunlight glisten on bark and bent-over grasses. The air smells of nothing – everything has been tumbled clean.

From my viewpoint on the deck opposite, my Gog looks lonely by himself. The two trees had stood so close to each other that their branches used to interdigitate, and in summer it was difficult to tell which one was which. Underground their network of roots would be doing the same – touching, communicating. Nuthatches would scuttle up and down their branches, and squirrels used them as bridges, regardless of which one belonged to each tree. Sun and rain touched them equally, as did wind. Until the day of the storm.

Maybe they both sprung from the same mother tree, even from the same year of harvest, as they're similar in size. Or more likely, both trees are the results of uneaten bounty hidden by the Screecher of the Woods, or Sgrech y Coed, the jay, its electric-blue wings and white rump flashing through the undergrowth as it searched for a spot amongst the thorny scrub to bury acorns. The jay's habit of burying them some distance from where they've been collected means that oak trees have spread outwards to the fields, and even uphill from the mother tree.

Magog has collapsed onto a bed of dry bracken, one of the only things that grow on this steep slope, pulling down a small hazel sapling in the process. Her silvery, bare branches have spread like the tentacles of a beached jellyfish and the splintered remains of her trunk thrust skywards, the exposed wood left naked and pale. Patches of yellow-brown moss cover the elephant greyness of the trunk, and lichen which usually drips from the branches, is now dropping onto the ground. A few curls of bleached polypody fern still cling to the vee of a branch.

Even though their host is dead, I hope all these will survive. I can't help but cry over the loss of something I thought of as a friend. Along with the notion that Gog must be missing her too. Once you give a name to something, it becomes something more.

It's the comparison with Dave that also resonates. A tall, big presence of a man, brought down by a collection of rogue cells, a whirlwind causing destruction through his body. In my mind's eye and in these early stages of grief, the similarity between the two is hard to ignore.

It's the middle of May and I look across at Gog and the fallen remains of Magog, still splayed across the hillside, from my vantage point on the deck on the opposite side of the bank. Dave built this deck a number of springs ago, my 'Gin deck' he called it, although it has to be said that more tea has been drunk here than gin. The deck is built at the side of the track that runs behind Shed field, where the old slurry pit used to be, and which leads from the farmyard to the lower fields – the old Cwm, and the new Cwm. Years ago, before we arrived, there was a spill from the slurry lagoon, causing cattle manure and water to pour down this side of the track, which then headed downwards towards the stream that trickles at the bottom of the valley, smothering all the low growing plants it touched. The area is still bare of trees, apart from an amazingly contorted, senior hawthorn, which must have just missed the spill, and whose branches are black and knobbled and covered with lichen, and a squat and spreading hazel tree.

The space is like a miniature amphitheatre, surrounded by trees higher up the slope, either side and opposite, and over the years has filled with bracken and bramble and willowherb. In March, a splash of snowdrops follows the path of the slurry spill and waterfall downwards, a bright white gash against the brown and emerging green of the scrub. The deck juts out above this open area and was built at this particular spot as Dave knew I loved looking out across the view, and if I could do it whilst sitting down with a pair of binoculars, even better. There's a 180-degree panoramic vision of it all, and it's perfect for watching birds as they fly and swoop and dart from tree to tree to tree across the gap. Even in the starkness of winter, or when its deluging rain, I always stop and look into the void, hoping to see something, anything.

In summer, a leaning ash tree casts its shade over the rear of the deck. It's always late into leaf and first in the wood to drop its still-green leaves. Handfuls of lime-green keys dangle at a reachable hand height, and stay on the tree all winter, slowly turning a chestnut-brown and rustling with the slightest breath of air. When the ash canopy is at its fullest, I lie on the bench and watch the leaves catching the sun and making patterns against the sky. Is there anything more lovely or anxiety-relieving than the whisper of leaves and shades of green through sunlight?

Framed within the viewpoint of my deck, the trees I can see whilst sitting on the old, worn bench are Gog and Magog right at the front, plus two ash, nine birch, one sycamore, three hawthorn, five hazel, and one magnificent beech. There's also one spindle, two horse chestnuts, one larch, and five evergreen conifers, which were included as part of a previous planting scheme and not native to here. Although the conifers shouldn't be in this wood, they may be the reason why goldcrests and the occasional firecrest can sometimes be seen, as both birds like to nest in conifers. Their nest is a hammock-like structure made of lichen, moss and cobwebs, spiders being a major part of their diet. They are both the tiniest of birds, approximately nine centimetres in length, and unless you get very close, are difficult to tell apart – the golden crown of the firecrest being more orange, with a black stripe through its eye and a white stripe above it. They are also noisy, and the high-pitched jingly zig-zig of a call reverberates through the woodland, so I've heard them more often than I've seen them. Some goldcrests are migratory and years ago people believed they travelled on the back of a woodcock or a short-eared owl, as it was thought they were too small to make the long journey from Scandinavia by themselves.

The sun feels warm against my face as I sip my tea and listen to the birds – chiffchaff, blackbird, blackcap, blue tit, great tit, plus the drumming from a greater spotted woodpecker lurking nearby. A speckled wood butterfly spirals up from the dimness of the flora below, banana yellow spots bright against the chocolate brown of its wings, and a cluster of soot-black St. Marks flies languorously glide above the rank grass, long legs dangling, wings a shimmering.

The enveloping trees are a warp and weft of different greens – mint, sage, apple, olive – all in various stages of leaf, although by August, the leaves will lose their spring newness and the colours will merge and blend into each other, as if copying a watercolour painting.

The wood is more than a collection of trees. You could put the exact same trees together in a different location, and it wouldn't feel the same. Place, and what it contains – wildlife, the soil, influence of the weather, history, myth, memories of people past and present – is everything. The presence or sense you feel in a wood is greater than the sum of its parts.

I focus on the apparent bareness of Magog, and notice that the small horizontal limb attached to her remaining standing trunk is scattered with tufts the colour of a new penny. They look like new leaves emerging, which maybe a small thing, but it may mean that Magog isn't dead at all.

It's a trek to find out – too steep to go as the crow flies – so the only option is to go back up the track and walk down the other side. This is nearly as steep, with over-hanging branches of hawthorn and hazel which catch in my hair, and my feet slip as I tread amongst twigs and leaves, the fallen memories of last year's summer. The emerging leaves of lesser celandines, which are invisible from my usual viewpoint, are also surprisingly slippery. Their flowers are beginning to open, their petals reflexing back on themselves, which, according to folklore, means it isn't going to rain. I love celandines and don't see them as weeds, as some do. Their buttercup-satin petals, a bright yellow with just a hint of green, glow in the sunlight, illuminating the ground. Higher up the bank, the apple-green trefoil leaves and the white veined-with-lilac bells of wood sorrel, or crinche cranche, rise amongst the moss growing on fallen branches. The flowers have a luminous quality against the dark of the floor of the wood and the bitter, lemon-zest tasting leaves make my mouth tingle as I nibble a heart-shaped corner. The leaves shut down at night and according to folklore are apparently eaten by cuckoos to clear their voices.

There's a small stream at the bottom of the slope. It meanders through boulders and rocks, some shot through with crystal, some smooth and cool to the touch, others craggy, with chunks gouged out of them, searching for the easiest way to reach the bottom of the cwm, which is what all watercourses do. In early summer, curls of scaly male fern unravel casting a feathery shadow over its surface whilst harts tongue ferns absorb as much moisture as they can. The stream runs through drifts of wild garlic, through primrosed banks, slips under the boughs of alder, willow and hazel, puddles with marsh marigold and flag iris before joining Nant Ceibwr, on its never-ending quest to find the sea.

Today, the stream is calm. It burbles and trickles, lying silently in pools of darkness in the hush of the wood, collecting in hollows created by fallen branches, where tiny insects circle aimlessly in the air above it, circle again and again like dust motes caught in the sun, and where the brown-green secret smell of a wood lies heavy. The stream in this upper part can disappear in a dry summer, leaving a pale, rocky path, the normally unseen bed exposed, the rocks drying and fading, but can torrent with gallons of frothing, churning, muddy water following days of rain.

Shadowing the course of the stream, the lime-green leaves of the golden saxifrage that highlight the shade of the path feel soft and springy under my feet. The plant vies with the similarly coloured moschatel, whose flowers on top of a miniature periscope-stem give it the name of the townhall clock plant. I jump across the narrowest part of the ditch and head up the other side of the slope, which is dominated by the cathedral-quiet of a huge beech tree, the so-called queen of the forest. She has a solid pillar of smooth grey trunk soaring into arms that spread and arch over the width of the path and beyond, and the emerging leaves have a wonderfully diffuse bright-green freshness, which flicker and dance with the sunlight. As yet the cover isn't strong enough to shade the ground, which is ankle deep in dry, brown leaves and the husks of empty beech masts, open like beige, origami petals, which rustle as I walk through them.

Further along, the path winds and dips through purple-blue billows of bluebells, which occupy the liminal space between wood and field and spread as far as the eye can see. Blue upon blue upon blue – a sign of an ancient woodland. It's hard not to stand on any of the plants, but when you do, there's a slight give, a slight crunch – the stem of a bluebell is hollow and filled with sap, which was once used to bind pages onto the spines of books. A faint smell of hyacinth drifts as I continue walking, and when I turn the corner, a patch of white gleams amongst the twisted roots of Gog. It's a small clump of white bluebells, which have the effect of making the blue ones bluer somehow. They are dainty and delicately pretty, and are probably quite rare, but for me, nothing is more beautiful than a blue one.

Further along the track is a badgers' sett. I don't walk down to it too often as I don't want to disturb them, but occasionally see them in the fields where they're digging for worms. They can move surprisingly fast when disturbed, a rippling run of black and white. They make a cacophony of noises – churrs, purrs, wails, chitters, snorts and yelps amongst others, which sound terrifying at night.

I turn downwards and half walk, half slide to reach Magog. The moss still clinging to its branches is dry to the touch, dry where it should be moist and springy. I have no idea if it's dead. Moss seems to grow on everything in this damp Welsh valley. I imagine, if I stood here long enough, it would soon grow on me.

Whereas moss tends to grow on the shady side of a tree, lichen prefers the sunny side and only grows where the air contains few pollutants. The lichen on Magog is the same colour as reindeer moss, a silvery sage, and looks like antlers on a deer with a few extra tendrils. It's abundant on most of the trees here, I can see it on Gog, on hawthorn, on blackthorn. It's called Evernia prunastri or oakmoss, and its musky, woody scent is the reason it's used in making perfume.

Lichens are supposed to be indicators of clean air and only grow a couple of millimetres a year, so some of them here must be years old. From what I've seen since living here, this wood – which covers about 20 acres and spreads through the north and eastern side of the farm – may be a remnant of a Celtic rainforest. Such habitats can be found along the western coastline of Wales, Scotland and England and are now fragmented and rare as a result of tree clearance and over-grazing. The plant indicators of this type of habitat are Polypody ferns, mosses and lichens and epiphytes – plants that grow on other trees due to the damp and humid conditions – and those abound here. Little islands of moss and fern on a sea of oak.

Standing amongst the trees, it's easy to see why there are so many myths and legends associated with them; the holy groves and walking place of the gods, inhabited with dryads, nymphs and centaurs. There is that sense of mystery, of magic about them, combined with the feeling they've been there for ever. Mixed with the haunting sense that one day they might not be, that time is running out for many woodlands.

There's something behind the remains of Magog, which I hadn't spotted from the deck. About twelve feet tall, it's a young Magog, with a grey striated trunk and rose-gold drops of leaves clasping thin branches. The sapling is leaning to the right, presumably so it could capture the maximum amount of light, as the bulk of the older tree would have blocked much of it out. Now Magog is no longer standing, it means this younger version will thrive. The pattern of regeneration in the world of the wood.

I sit on one of Magog's fallen branches and place a hand on the wood. It's rough, pitted, dry, and already the bark is beginning to lift in a few places – it's becoming a home for new insects. The earthy smell of years of death and regrowth rises from where my feet have disturbed the ground, ground normally tracked by foxes, badgers, the occasional rabbit. I look up at the jagged remains of the trunk, standing ten foot or so, piercing the air. It really did split like a matchstick. But growing on one side, the same colour as the new oak sapling, a ruff of leaves is stretching outwards, feeling for life.

~ *A Decision to Leave* ~

As much as I loved being on the farm, in the immediate aftermath of Dave's death, I wanted to get as far away from it as possible. Memories of him were everywhere. He'd worked on every part of the farmhouse, the cottage, as well as in the fields. Every inch of the place held some sort of memory of him. I thought about selling the farm, moving away. It was too lonely, too expensive. And then lockdown happened, and I couldn't do anything except walk and think.

The decision to leave was a hard one and my feelings kept on changing. It wasn't a quick decision; I just didn't know if it was the right one. I made lists of pros and cons. Reasons to leave – too far from family, too lonely, too expensive, too much work, my health, safety (my dogs had pulled me over one evening, resulting in me suffering a mild concussion and there was no one around to help), too many memories of Dave. Reasons to stay – friends nearby, the woods, the fields, the birds and animals, the peace. Memories of Dave.

I hadn't fallen in love with Penbanc straight away, it took a while. I missed family and friends; the house needed so much work. But the land always drew me in. The trees, the fields, the distant glimpse of the sea, were always there to go to when things weren't going too well.

Dave and I moved in September and the first full day on the farm is one I remember clearly. It was one of those rare, soft days, with a touch of bittersweet, as you know the dark of winter is on its way. Sitting outside on the low wall that edged the garden, the only sound was that of the birds. In the evening, we walked the boundaries of the land and the woods, now ours for a while, and wondered how long it would take before we remembered what the field names were, and which field was where.

It took a while for me to become familiar with them all. I didn't walk them as Dave did, checking on the sheep with the sheepdogs every day, I couldn't walk my dogs in the fields that held sheep, and in the summer, I couldn't walk in my favourite part, the lower fields, as neighbours kept their cattle there – I'm scared of cows after being chased by a herd years before.

It seems strange that I only got to know the land more after Dave died, mainly because eight months later, lockdown began, which meant I had every opportunity to walk every inch of it, investigate those hidden areas I'd walked past as I was always in a rush to be somewhere else. Those unknown spaces became places, places I got to know well.

I was able to sit, to think. I came to love the place more, even though it was brim-full of grief. And how lucky was I to have such a place. Being amongst the birds, the trees, soothed and calmed. Working in the garden again helped. Plus, Dave had loved Penbanc and had never wanted to be anywhere else. Lockdown put all thoughts of leaving on hold.

But over the next year, various happenings made me think about it again. Dave's absence became a kind of presence. The time came for one daughter who had been living in the cottage to leave and one had a baby who I was unable to see much of due to lockdown. My other daughter became pregnant with twins, also living away. And although I'm quite a solitary person, I became lonely. Things started to go wrong with the farm, things that Dave could have dealt with easily. I wasn't a farmer, a carpenter, a woodsman, a welder or a roofer. I wasn't even strong enough for the most basic of things, the rheumatoid arthritis I suffered from annoyingly affecting my joints and energy. Although offers to help had been given when Dave was ill, apart from my nearest neighbour who was ever helpful, these faded away and I didn't like to keep asking. Paid work was also hard to find during lockdown. The farm started to crumble. A bit like my joints. I began to dread what would go wrong next.

The final thing that made me decide to leave was a storm. The north wind battering against the window brought other sounds – the nails-down-a-chalk-board screech of metal on metal, plus a thump of metal on wood. Outside, in the half-light and driving rain, I could see a piece of corrugated metal roofing lifting with each gust of wind that hit the barn, another piece just holding on with one screw. I needed to do something about this one as the weight and sharp edges of it could injure someone or an animal severely if it flew off. Already soaked by the rain, after many attempts, I managed to pull the heavy metal sheet from the barn side and dropped it onto the floor, cutting my hand in the process. The other piece of roofing would have to stay unsafe until I could find someone else to fix it. It would take a while.

It didn't take much to make me cry, not then. So I did, standing in the rain, wet through. I'd had enough.

Even though I had made a decision, I still wondered if it was the right one. I kept procrastinating about when to put the farm on the market. There was so much clearing to be done, especially in the farm buildings which were full of farm paraphernalia. I decided to sell or get rid of as much as I could and then contact an estate agent.

I sold Dave's New Holland tractor, which he'd loved, as well as all the attachments that went with it – harrows, pallet fork, rollers, a front-end loader, plus other things that I couldn't identify. Sold his sheep trailer, his low-loading trailer, the sheep race and handling equipment, stop gates, hurdles, all implements for shearing, garden rotavator, strimmers, chainsaws, mowers, log splitters, battery chargers, ladders. I kept the sit-on mower and the quadbike. There were piles and boxes of hammers, chisels, saws, drills, drill bits, nails, screws, files, spanners in his lockable shed, the Dutch barn and the machinery shed. Plus, three orange cement mixers. Why have one when you can have three?

I started to make a small collection of things I might need. A couple of hammers and saws, screws and nails still in packets rather than in buckets – so many of these had become rusty by being left out in the damp and salty air, and I hadn't thought to collect them all and put them inside. And when this was done, I asked around to see if anyone would like to come and take anything for free, rather than let things go to waste.

Some neighbours and friends of neighbours did come, but even when most things that could still be used were taken, there was a lot left to clear. I filled a dozen skips over the next six months, and when this was done there were no practical reasons to delay calling the estate agent. Apart from an emotional attachment which I knew was always going to be there whether I lived in Penbanc or not. I just hoped that I would leave some sort of mark on the place, just as I knew it would leave its mark on me.

~ *A Beltane Walk* ~

The chatter of sparrows outside my bedroom window woke me up at five thirty. I got up and drew the curtains to peer outside, shivering a little. A sky of speckled blue. No rain yet. An early morning smell of dew and earth. The sparrows were strung out in a line along the electric wire that runs alongside the farmhouse, announcing a new day. A noise unheard by me caused them to fly towards the concrete yard to join the rest of their flock. Two swallows took their place, twittering and chirping, tail streamers dangling. At eye height, they were the closest I'd ever get, their iridescent blue-black back and wings and a metal-red throat contrasting with their cream chest. Opposite, a pied wagtail was running up and down the U shape of the rusting corrugated iron barn roof, tail flicking up and down, whilst a magpie of similar colouring but much larger size stood on the roof ridge, chest puffed, looking this way and that as if on look-out duty.

Although I enjoy observing the different perspective of the yard from the bed, looking down on everything, not just at foot level, I was too awake to get back into it this morning, so a walk it was. It seemed fitting on this day of bright fire, a day of new beginnings. I would walk in the woods to hear the awakening of the birds. Dave had loved the fields, but I loved the woods, the secret, all-encompassing beauty of them all. And one of the things I loved about the woods, was that I was superfluous to them. The wood would carry on regardless of whether I was involved with it or not.

If you go to the side of the neglected cowshed, where the concrete is cracked and uneven, and where the nettle and bramble and couch grass abound, there's a track leading downwards towards the lower fields. It's a person-and-a-dog-width wide and threatening to become narrower. You have to skirt around a self-sown elder sapling that's growing in the middle of the path, which I should pull out, but am loath to do so as an elder tree is reputed to protect a house from evil spirits. Small outcrops of rock merge with tussocks of tough-as-twine rye grass, and you need to be careful where you place your feet, especially when the blackberry starts to wander where it shouldn't.

The path runs parallel to Parc Dai on the left, whilst on the right, the wooden deck stretches into the space. It's in full view of the sun on this early morning and the surrounding air is full of tiny flying insects, caught in a net of sunbeams trickling through the trees. They're too small for me to see what they are but I have no need or wish to know. They fizz and sparkle, endlessly rising, falling, circling, little oscillations of light and it's as if the light is emanating from within them not reflected. I want to go and sit on the bench near to them but have no wish to disturb this illusion of magic. I'll sit on the way back up.

I walk through the small gateway which no longer has a gate, brushing through the dew-damp fronds of fern and grass and stems of rosebay willow herb, yet to flower. Along the left side, an old wall, built of slate in the local herringbone method and used where the stone is thin and prone to splintering, supports this side of the green lane, grass now growing amongst the vertical coping stones. Pennywort, *Umbilicus rupestris*, a type of stonecrop, clings to gaps in the walls, its rosettes of leaves dimpled in the centre which is why the plant is also called navelwort. The fleshy leaves are edible, with a taste similar to a lettuce but I don't like the rubbery texture of them, so they stay safe on the wall.

Towering above, a hawthorn, *Crataegus monogyna*, is just coming into bloom, and in a few weeks will be dripping blossoms of white tinged with pink. Hawthorn, Queen of the May, or the Fairy Tree – as fairies live in them – is a tree that symbolises Beltane and stands at the entrance to the otherworld. The flowers have an almond smell, stronger at evening, but can become putrid when the flowers start to decay. I remember picking May flowers to bring into the house when I was a child as they were so pretty until my grandmother threw them outside as they were reputed to signify a death in the household. I pick a polished, new leaf to chew on as I'm passing underneath. It tastes nothing like the bread and cheese it's supposed to taste like, but I keep trying, in case one day it does.

The rowan, or mountain ash, *Sorbus aucuparia*, standing just down from it, blooms more subtly, with flowers of a soft cream. It's another tree that offers protection against witches. As I walk downwards, the trees form a translucent green archway as I pass underneath them. They mirror the cloisters of Gloucester Cathedral, the paleness of birch and ash replacing the vaulting pillars and buttresses of limestone. Buds on the sycamore trees are emerging, fat, magnolia buds of prawn pink, which the honeybees love, one of their main food sources this time of the year. The canopy sometimes thrums with the hum of them. People often look down on sycamores, tree weeds, as they call them, but I love them. Introduced by the Romans, they were more generally planted in the 1700s, often to shelter and protect farmhouses as they are tolerant of salty winds, or as specimen trees due to the speed with which they grow. A sycamore can live up to 400 years old, spreading easily due to their 'helicopter' seeds, or samaras which can spiral away from the mother tree a good distance. Sycamore wood is pale and fine grained and is used to make Welsh love spoons. A little further along is a favourite tree, another sycamore, which has an almost perfect symmetrical shape. It sits at the bottom of the small ravine, so I look right into the green heart of it, my magic faraway tree.

On the opposite bank, a huge goat willow leans downwards. It has lost many of its lower branches over the last few years, but those left are full of soon-to-be released seed capsules. For a few days, the air will be full of gossamer threads, swamping every surface so the whole area becomes a world of silvery-white.

Flitting and hopping from one branch or twig to another, the long-tailed tits, or titmice, acrobat through the woodland searching for food. Calling to each other – a 'see-see-see'– they are always in a group, a swirl of plaster-pink, black and white with a flash of a tail. They are the prettiest of creatures.

Passing the foot of the red kite oak, the bluebells point the way downwards, where violet, lavender, lapis and cobalt pools lap against the white carpeting stars of wild garlic, pungent when you place your foot amongst them. The trees thin as you reach the bottom of the slope and meet up with the field, the Old Cwm, a secret, magical place, where the oaks are replaced by willow and alder and birch, which paddle in the soft water of the stream and shepherd the quietly flowing water toward the sea.

The stream trickles through two fields before joining with Nant Ceibwr and it twists and bends around boulders of white crystal, and grey slabs of stone. In the middle of the second field, the soil here is softer, so the force of the winter water has carved out a miniature ox-bow lake as it finds the path of least resistance. A fallen oak tree, still alive but recumbent, resembles a large Ikadabuki bonsai, with vertical branches rising from the fallen trunk. It lies across half of the stream and has created a natural dam, causing the silt and soil being carried seawards to build up behind it. This new piece of land gets bigger every year and is being populated by wild garlic, red campion and wood melick. The new angle caused by the tree has also caused the water to flow faster so more of the bank is disappearing – the soil needs to be dug out to halt the loss of the field but that's something I'm not able to do.

The flow is tranquil this morning, with only the sound of water plinking against pebbles and stone and I walk alongside of it to where the bank drops slightly so I can paddle in the water. One side of the bank is covered with primrose and violets and the other with wild garlic, whilst in a damp corner, at eye height, a yellow flag iris pierces upwards through the pink stars of ragged robin which meander around the margins. This is the only place on the farm where it grows.

The water is ice-cold, so I only stay in it for a couple of minutes until my feet are pleasantly numb. I do what I always do which is to break off a twig and drop it into the water and wonder how long it would take before it arrives at the sea at Ceibwr, which is something I have no way of knowing. The first years we were here, Dave and I talked about walking or kayaking down the watercourse to see how long it would take, if we could do so without meeting any barrier, of course. What would we see at stream height, what might we find, on this unusual journey? Something else I have no way of knowing.

In the corner of this field, a small group of alders, *Alnus glutinosa*, are helping to stabilise the water bank as these trees are able to withstand being submerged in shallow water. So-called pioneer trees, surviving in barren areas, they are nitrogen fixers, as they extract nitrogen from the air and the bacterium *Farnkia alni* present in their roots converts it to compounds the tree can use to enrich the soil around them. Alder, or Fearn, is the magical tree of Bran the Blessed, is sacred to the druids, and symbolises the fourth month of the Ogham calendar. With its feet in the earth and water and its arms in the air, the tree was considered to be a gateway to the otherworld. Alder woods are known as carrs and were seen as places of secrecy and mystery. Alder wood is a vivid orange when first cut and can appear as if it is bleeding, which caused people to fear such trees. This wood is used to make clogs and lock gates – most of Venice is constructed on alder trunks. As the pith is easily removed, whistles were made from alder shoots and used to entice air elementals.

Passing under the trees, green knobbly young fruits, like small pinecones hang on the end of small branches, alongside female wine-red cones and brown-yellow male catkins. The green dye produced from this fruit was believed to colour the clothes of fairies.

In the next field, the water is shallower and wider and gurgles over the stones. Trees arch overhead so the stream is a mix of water and shadows. A dipper visits here sometimes, a plump bird with a cocked tail like a wren, flashing white breast against conker-brown, nodding and bobbing amongst the pebbles. When underwater, this brown appears mercury silver due to air bubbles trapped amongst its feathers. Dippers, *Cinclus cinclus*, or the 'bird of the torrent' have a third eye, a nictitating membrane, which they can close so they can see underwater, and act like a bird version of a windscreen wiper, cleaning and moistening its eye. They have high levels of haemoglobin levels in their blood which enable the bird to store oxygen when diving, whilst their wings act like flippers, and their long toes and claws enable them to grip onto the riverbed. Dippers are our only aquatic songbirds, and their song is surprisingly loud, a metallic jumble of sounds – it has to be loud so it can be heard above the noise of the rushing water. The jizz of the bird means it's as one with the stream – brown, black and silver dappled, a fast moving, burbling entity. No dipper is feeding here today.

I skirt past another fallen tree, this time an ash, gently disintegrating into the water. This is technically the extent of our land, but I can walk further if I stay close to the bank. Barbed wire has been strung along the tree line and it's been here a while as each tree is attempting to grow around it. I've cut the wire on my side; I cut any I can find. I've never understood the cruel, lazy, and pointless practise of hammering wire into a tree, and have a loathing of barbed wire used needlessly.

The wood is full to the brim with birdsong and it's difficult to tell one bird from the other. I stand still for a moment, closing my eyes to focus. Robin, blackbird, chiffchaff. A scattering of wrens. A waft of earth and garlic. A suthering of wind in the trees.

A few years ago and a little way along, I caught a sliver of brightness in the water just here. The sun flickering shadows made it difficult to work out what it was, but further along where the tree canopy lessened and the sun lit the water, I could see clearly. Grey-brown and eel-like, each two hands widths long, a cluster of lampreys swayed slowly with the flow of the water, in and out of the shadows, glistening where the sun touched. These pre-historic fish attach to the rocks with a suckered mouth rather than a jaw, bodies held together with cartilage not bone. There are three species of lamprey and I'm not sure what these are – I can't get close to see them in more detail. They were once considered a food delicacy throughout Europe, and the Queen's coronation pie was made using them in 1953. I have no desire to eat one and I'm relieved I'm not still in the water.

The neighbours say that sewin, the local, migratory sea trout, have been seen in Nant Ceibwr, as far up as here, but I have never seen one. Apart from the lampreys, I have never seen any fish in this water.

I leave the cool of the wood and turn back across the field. There's a small rocky outcrop where a couple of sheep's-bit scabious plants, with lilac-blue thrift-like flowers, grow alongside a patch of lousewort, *Pedicularis sylvatica*. This has mid-pink flowering nettle-like flower spikes, growing from a creeping mat of leaves and is hemi-parasitic in that its roots attach themselves to the roots of other plants so it can extract minerals and water from them. It was so called because it was believed the plant infected sheep with lice. Or that it was used to prevent an infestation of them. Like the ragged robin growing in the damp soil near the stream, this is the only place on the farm that lousewort grows. Some plants, like some people, have specific places where they can thrive.

The Old Cwm is the remains of an ancient meadow, sheep-shorn in the early summer and left to get on with it for the rest of the year. It lies wet in winter so is left farm animal free. As the field is unreachable by a tractor, it's never been ploughed or fertilised or had a new ley planted, which is a bonus. Red campion, meadowsweet, early purple orchid, field buttercup, yarrow, jostle amongst sweet vernal, Yorkshire fog and false oat grass. When the meadowsweet, or the Queen of the meadow, is high and just coming into flower, I make a tea with freshly picked blossoms, which are the colour of frothed cream and smell of almonds and summer and taste the same. Meadowsweet has many uses in herbalism, and I use it because it reduces inflammation as it contains salicylic acid, an ingredient of aspirin. It is also used in the making of mead and was sacred to the druids.

In summer, silver washed fritillaries, *Argynnis paphia*, meander through the margins of the wood and field, circling and zigzagging through bramble and thistles. From a distance they look like large orange butterflies, but up close, their tangerine wings are dotted with brown whilst the underside is a pale green, overlaid with iridescent silvery streaks. The caterpillars feed on violets which are often found under oak trees. They are striking, beautiful butterflies and these were the first fritillaries I had ever seen.

I take off my jacket as I walk back up the slope and am out of breath by the time I reach the top, even though I do this walk daily. It's a good excuse to sit on the bench for a while. Sometimes I lie upon it and stare up at the clouds. As a child I'd see animals, mythological creatures, imagined fairy castles forming within them. Whenever on a plane, I'd have my face pressed to the window, wanting to be immersed amongst the clouds, to see them from above, from inside, not just from below. To me, they weren't just harbingers of the weather, more like another layer of being. Now I still see animals, mythological creatures, imagine fairy castles, watch as they form and roll and re-form, some moving fast, some slower, see them appear, fade, disappear, regrow. So intent was I at making pictures in the canvas above me one day, it took a while to realise that the anxiety always curling around my edges had eased slightly. Which gave me a reason to make time to watch clouds.

There are not many clouds to watch today, only a few wisps of white moving slowly westwards. The air is still, devoid now of flying insects, the sky a larimar blue filtered through the spider threads of white. Every shade of green spreads out before me – the human eye can see more varieties of green than any other colour. Small brown birds flutter and tumble and soar from branch to branch. A male blackcap sits half-hidden through an elder. There's an alarum of a great tit in the scrub. Above me, a buzzard circles high, dancing through the clouds.

~ *The Lane* ~

The driveway from the front door to the top of our lane is a third of a mile long and people only come down it to see me or to deliver something. Or if they're lost. The mail gets delivered to an American style box which is situated at the junction of the lane and the road that leads to Moylegrove, so I walk up the steep slope to check for post every day and have done for the last ten years. The box itself lies in wait in the blackthorn hedge, which is ready to attack anyone who gets too close, so I often take secateurs with me to trim the blackthorn as I don't want myself or the postman to get stabbed by its vicious spikes. Tiny pieces can break-off under your skin and turn septic, so not getting too near them is best (unless it's autumn and you're wanting to pick the sloes for gin).

We had to replace the cracked and pitted drive when we moved in, as half of it ended up in a moraine-like mass of mud and shale and gravel outside the farmhouse following the first winter storm. Two lines of concrete now run from top to bottom, leaving a narrow strip of green in-between, a strip that has become colonised with seeds carried down by the rain, the water pouring down the new track as if someone has pulled a plug.

Where the overhanging hedge casts a shadow, the strip of green is of dog violet, self-heal, grass, and where the sun shimmies through the gaps, the green is of daisy, wild strawberry, black medick, plantain. Red clover bridges the space and spreads between the two, handily growing opposite the beehives which lie halfway along the track. Its common name is honeystalks, because you can suck a tiny drop of nectar from a floret, something I remember doing as a child. Red clover's flowers are more pink than red, and what appears to be a flower is in fact an inflorescence, a cluster of skyward facing tubular florets of cerise and rose-pink. In the shade, they stretch their necks to follow the sun, whilst on the dry shale side they bask and sprawl sideways. The bees seem to love them, almost falling out of their hive to lie and fly amongst the blooms, and although the flower tube is sometimes too long for the honeybee to reach into to collect nectar, they have no difficulty in collecting pollen. This collects on their heads, and the bee then uses its front legs to transfer the brown pollen into the pollen basket on their hind legs, which looks like a saddlebag when it's full.

It's relaxing to watch the bees foraging, and the garden is full of flowers I've planted for them. Along with the wild plants already present such as ivy, sycamore, willow and apple, there's something for every season – crocus, snowdrop, hellebore, foxglove, honeysuckle, single roses, lavender, buddleia, marjoram, thyme, raspberry, sedum, mahonia. Apparently, ten bee-loads of pollen are needed to produce one worker bee, which is a lot of pollen.

Last summer, I made lemonade from the red clover flowers. You have to pick them before the pompom flowers turn brown, then simmer them with honey, letting the liquid steep overnight before adding the juice of a lemon. It turns the colour of a ripe apricot and has a delicate, floral taste. It's supposedly full of isoflavones, vitamin C, potassium and calcium and is thought to act as diuretic, an expectorant, and to help cleanse the liver. I just like the fact that I can source the flowers and the honey from outside my front door.

The track runs between two fields, Parc Cartws, or First field on the right on the way up, and Parc Main or Quarry field on the left. Main means thin, and it is a narrow piece of land, and the English name is self-explanatory – there's a small shale quarry in the top part of it. The sides are steep, but as yet, no animal has fallen in. Half of the quarry is surrounded by gorse bushes, which shine a neon yellow for months and flood the hollow with a Hawaiian tropic smell on a warm day, and is the summer home to stonechats, meadow pipits and yellowhammers. First field is also self-explanatory as it's the first field you see when you come down the lane. I call it that rather than Cartws, as that is what we called it when we arrived, not then knowing its original name. Cartws means Cart house, so there must have been one somewhere on the field, although there's no evidence of one now. Old maps show the field was divided into two until the hedge was pulled out years ago.

There's a cattle grid at the top of the track which is supposed to prevent animals from escaping or entering. It doesn't: one of our sheep, a cross between a Welsh mountain and a Lleyn, regularly jumped, rolled or tightroped along the metal bars, sometimes with a lamb in tow, and a neighbour's sheep regularly appeared to eat the garden I'd planted for the bees. We'd planned to fill in the grid, worried that creatures such as hedgehogs or frogs would fall into it and be unable to get out, but it was another job we never got around to. Checking for potential casualties became a daily habit although I had no plan on how to remove anything if they did fall. In summer, the drain is colonised by plants that enjoy the damp coolness – the emerald green, smooth-to-the-touch birds nest fern, unravelling curls of bracken, and foxgloves, which get decapitated every time they became tall enough to peer over the edge. Dave placed a cut scaffold plank across one side to walk across, as I had visions of my foot getting stuck.

Once over the cattle grid, you can turn right to Moylegrove, or left which takes you towards the road to Nevern. There are five gateways in a rough circle – ours, leading into Cartws field; next doors field, Pwll Hedydd, to the left; opposite, two more fields that used to belong to Penbanc – Rhos Isaf and Rhos Fach; and centrally, heading west, Parc Stand, a path that leads to the viewpoint at Crugiau Cemaes. Rhos means moorland, but the field shows little evidence of this now. Years of soil improvement have made it a rich pasture for cattle and sheep.

When I reach the five gates, I know without thinking, which way the wind is blowing depending on where it touches the skin on my face. Today, a hint of a breeze is touching my left cheek, so it's arriving from the south. When the wind blows strongly from the east, the gates sing, an otherworld pan-pipe sound. Although the gates are made from metal, each is made slightly differently, so hum at different pitches. It was difficult to work out where the noise was coming from the first time I heard it and it scared the dogs, but I like it, like the evidence of wind as a presence. The wind has its own character here, has moulded and bullied the landscape and the trees.

Some days, when reaching this spot, I just stand and close my eyes. Feel the sun, the wind, the rain. Absorb the atmosphere. Listen. You can hear more when you close your eyes, all the other senses compensating for a temporary loss of vision. Today, a blackbird is singing; a lamb is calling; a swallow twitters and chirps; a tractor rattles in the distance, and there's a faint smell of grass touched by the sun. I can almost hear it growing. I wonder about the people who have walked this same path before me, when the lane was earth, not concrete. Did they do the same? Or were they too busy trying to earn a living from the land to stand and close their eyes.

Taking the left turn towards Nevern, I feel I know the essence of this lane now, after all these years of walking along it. I'm familiar with its twists and bends, know the exact place where you can see the sea between a gap in the hawthorn hedge on a clear day; the way the camber falls to the right on the first left hand corner, eroded by the relentless Welsh rain funnelling through, and on the same bend, how the webs of the spiders soften the spikes of the holly hedge as they abseil between them, only visible when the early morning dew clings to each thread, outlining each one in precise detail; know the spot where the heady smell of evening honeysuckle lies strongest. How, in early summer, the green corridor running through it becomes sprinkled with the stars of cinquefoil and chickweed. That around the next corner, where a section of the field is left to seed, you can smell the grass drying or see the citrine flash of a yellowhammer, and over the next gate where the land lies higher, hear the sunshine-in-a-song call of the skylarks as they rise and fall.

On this late May morning, the sea is a bright, pewter line, the sun August-hot. The cow parsley is shoulder high, touching the almond scented flowers of the hawthorn which drip downwards like icing on a cake. The lane is afroth with white blossom framed against the pale blueness of a sky ribboned with a nectarine blush. On the northern side of the lane, a few bluebells fade silently, whilst cleaver clambers through woodruff. The bank which supports the hedge is head-high here which offers a different perspective – some of the plants growing on the almost vertical slope are almost unnoticeable at ground level. Wood sage is one such plant. Overall, its crinkled and hairy-to-touch leaves are grass-green so the plant is easily overlooked, but close up, the tiny pale-yellow flowers with maroon striped tongues resemble miniature snapdragons and they cling tight against the upright, woody stem. Unlike culinary sage, wood sage has no smell although the insects seem to like it. Just below and free from the confines of the ground, wild strawberry drips red. Even though a few cars pass through the lane, I can't resist picking a few berries to eat – all their flavour is concentrated in one tiny mouthful, a miniscule pop of sweetness.

Amongst the bracken and pinking sorrel, a wren scuttles. Last July, five hatchlings were near the same spot, trilling and ticking and chittering before I saw them, such a big sound for such diminutive creatures. They hid and dived amongst the undergrowth, and apart from their cocked tails, resembled insects more than birds. One took a chance and attempted a maiden flight, balancing on a fern frond, which barely moved.

Around the next corner, the hedges are higher and the varieties of flowers less. The hedges are a mix of hawthorn, blackthorn, hazel, entwined with ivy, honeysuckle, dog rose, bramble and old man's beard. There's also an oak, which tries to grow taller every year but is doomed to fail due to the farmer's hedge-cutting policy, and a willow, whose olive-green spread is wider than its height, and which loses a few branches every winter, on two occasions blocking the lane.

Mounds of red campion are collapsing into the road. They seem to be the most common flower around here, taking advantage of any available space. Their flowers are everywhere – the lane, the corners of the fields, the vegetable garden, and some have seeded in my pots that flank the front door. I've even seen one flowering in December. The five deeply lobed petals are the colour of candyfloss, and the fairies reputedly use the flowers to protect their honey stores, which is why it's considered unlucky to pick them. Their Welsh name is Blodyn Neidr, which means snake flower, and the seeds were used traditionally to treat snakebite. Along parts of the lane, red campion, bluebells and cow parsley thread and weave and flower together and how beautiful they look. Nature makes the best arrangements.

In the field where lambs are jostling their mothers for food, a comma butterfly is sunning itself on the fencepost. It's easy to identify with its jagged wing edges. When the wings are closed, the butterfly resembles a dead leaf – which must be an advantage – and I can just make out the small white comma mark on its hindwing, but when the wings open, they're a rich orange colour, with tortoiseshell markings. The comma is a rare example of a butterfly that's increasing in numbers. Numbers declined drastically when its preferred foodplant, the hop, became less available due to the decline in hop farming. It adapted its preference by eating nettles, which are widespread, and has therefore been able to spread throughout the country. It's a lovely creature and they are one of the most common butterflies on the farm, but the days when you walked through a meadow disturbing clouds of comma, meadow brown and gatekeeper, and when the buddleia in the garden was covered by peacocks, tortoiseshells, and painted ladies are gone. I get excited to see one butterfly now.

I stand and watch the lambs for a while. After years of looking after my own, it's lovely to watch them play in the sunshine, without worrying about whether they're getting enough food, if they're healthy, or if a fox is going to get one. These are making the most of a small rise in the field, by playing king of the castle. They run and bound, twisting sideways in the air, jumping with all four feet together, race to one side of the field and then the other, their undocked tails wriggling. The ewes ignore them for a time now – the lambs are big enough and know enough to come and feed when they want to, butting and sometimes almost lifting their poor mothers off the ground, especially when twins feed at the same time. One ewe calls repeatedly in the corner – it's the call of a sheep that's lost her lamb. As they're not mine, I ignore the urge to climb the gate and look for it. Hopefully, it's one of the lambs in the pack helter-skeltering around the field. The unique smell of warm sheep; of lanolin, of wool, of dung, drifts over the gate. These ewes will need shearing soon, so flies won't be able to lay eggs in their wool. Maggots can kill a sheep in a day.

I turn away and continue walking downwards towards the road. Here, you can turn left to go to Cardigan town through Glanrhyd, or right to go to the viewpoint, Bayvil and onto Nevern. Opposite, lies the crenellated ridge of the Preseli mountains, with Frenni Fawr rising on the left. Today, they are as clear as if someone had outlined them with a pencil. The land below rests green after the recent rain, overlaid with darker shadows which chase across the fields as the clouds scud over the sun.

~ *The Rose* ~

*'There is simply the rose; it is perfect
in every moment of its existence'.*

(Ralph Waldo Emerson)

It's Midsummer day and the uncut grasses at the end of the lane are already losing their spring freshness and show hints of tawny, fawn, russet. The white umbels of cow parsley are heavy-green with seeds whilst the leaning spires of foxgloves have replaced the bubble-gum pink of red campion. Young blue-tits acrobat and dive through the collapsing undergrowth and in the dark of a holly bush, a robin sings quietly to itself.

June is the month for roses and the unusual spell of days of sun has been perfect for them. In the early morning and when the earth cools at the end of the day, their smell of musk, myrrh and orange-blossom, hangs heavy in the stillness, drifting through the shadows cast by the trees and the buildings.

I love roses, especially the old historical varieties. They can be difficult to grow – many flower only once in the summer, they can be untidy in the garden and have a habit of collapsing without support – but all are beautiful and most carry a delicious scent. And as well as being beautiful, they have stories behind their names, for example *Rosa Mundi*, the so-called Rose of the World, reputedly named after fair Rosamund, the mistress of Henry II and one of the roses that symbolises the end of the War of the Roses. The white rose was the emblem of the House of York, whilst red represented the House of Lancaster. Mundi is a mix of the two colours – imagine raspberry jam swirled into vanilla ice cream, the pattern different every time you do it.

I've dug, chiselled, and potted over one hundred varieties here, have planted them in borders, to cover walls and buildings and over trees.

Some have taken a dislike to the damp Welsh weather and thin soil and have refused to grow, but others have thrived.

Ispahan, a perfection in Schiaparelli pink, is collapsing gracefully over the overgrown box hedge under the weight of her flowers. They have quartered swirls and curls that feel like silk, and some have a tiny, green button eye that becomes visible when the flowers are fully open. The blooms have a quality that make them appear to glow at dusk and have a delicious, sweet perfume, called Old Rose by the experts in such things. Ispahan comes from the city of Isfahan in Persia – now Iran – so the heat and dryness of the last week is ideal for her. She is a damask rose and was introduced into Europe around 1894, although other damask roses were brought back earlier by returning crusaders. Her flowers last for about six weeks, which is a long time for an old rose, and she is glorious when in full bloom.

In the opposite border, outlined by the dark of a conifer, Hebe's lip trembles in the slight breeze. Her ivory tissue-paper petals are encircled with a cherry-red lip liner that fades as the sun kisses them, which then fold gently over the starburst of buttercup-yellow stamens nestling in her centre. She arches delicately over the mauve spikes of lavender and has a Titania's bower smell of musk surrounding her – strong and heady, lilac mixed with violets.

Souvenir de Madame Leonie Viennot is pulling herself out of the large container I planted her in and is trying to escape over the roof of the barn. She is blowsy and extravagant and throws herself over every surface she touches with abandonment. Her flowers are the colour of the blush on a ripe peach and smell like raspberries freshly picked. She was very popular during the 1920s, I imagine as a cut flower, and was often grown in a conservatory as she can be temperamental in cold gardens.

On the sunny side of the barn, Mutablis winds her way amongst the orange-brown of a carex grass and allows the cerise-flowered viticella clematis Etoile Rose to scramble through her. Mutablis originates from

China and when in flower looks like a bush covered with apricot, crimson and fuchsia butterflies. Mutablis is the Latin for change and that is what her flowers do – they start one colour and over a few days, change to another. The five-petaled silk-like blooms only have a faint smell but I forgive her for this minor fault because in full bloom, she is simply stunning. There is a garden in Italy – La Landriana – where the owner has planted 300 of these roses amongst grasses to create a rose forest, a forest full of flower-butterflies. I hope to visit one day.

Souvenir de la Malmaison grows to about four feet tall and her leaves will be spotted with black by the time she has finished flowering as the usual dampness of the Welsh weather doesn't agree with her. Souvenir was created in 1843 in Lyon in France and named after Empress Josephine's famous rose garden at Chateau de Malmaison in France where Josephine lived with Napoleon Bonaparte. Between 1804 and 1814, this contained the largest collection of roses in the world having over 200 varieties.

Interestingly, despite being at war, Napoleon allowed the transport of roses from England, and shipments of roses were able to cross the blockades. As she died in 1814, Josephine never got to see this sumptuous variety, with its blush and powder pink cupped blooms, that fold into four quarters around a central eye like the encircling leaves of a cabbage – it was named in memory of her. I'm hoping this 'Queen of delights' will grow taller so I can smell her rich, heady, spicy-hyacinth perfume at head height, rather than having to bend down, and even if she only produces one flower a year, it will be worth it.

As special and beautiful as these old roses are, the real stars of June are the wild roses: the dog rose, the briar rose, the field rose. All along the lane you can see them climbing, sprawling, cascading and clambering into trees, hooking themselves through the ivy they share a space with. In Cromlech field, one has draped itself over an elder tree, all afroth with cream, and is entwined with a butter-yellow honeysuckle, by a happy coincidence, all three flowering at the same time. The colours of these roses vary. Some are the palest of pinks, that drift to white as they age, others hint of madder, salmon, watermelon. All with a central boss of the most golden of stamens. Some have a sweet, floral, musky aroma, whilst others carry no scent at all. In autumn, trails and streamers of scarlet hips adorn the hedgerows.

I made rose hip syrup one year as it's supposed to prevent colds. One teaspoon contains half the vitamin C needed for a child's daily intake, the hips containing 20 percent more vitamin C than oranges. The process is fiddly and sticky and the resulting peach coloured, silky syrup has a subtle tropical tang with a hint of almond, but I left the hips for the birds the following years.

A wild rose has decided to grow in a border at the side of the house. I decided to let it do its thing and now the straggling bush is the same height as me and twice as wide. The flowers are cerise fading through the palest of pinks to cream, then white, and each of the five petals have a slight dip in the centre so they resemble a heart. The perfume of the individual flowers isn't strong but when you stand up close, the surrounding air breathes rose.

Last year, I found two other seedlings, and carefully teased their fragile roots from the thin soil they'd decided to settle in. I planted one on the final resting place of my beloved dog Rosie. She's buried underneath the tree where she used to wait for a squirrel to appear, remaining convinced to the end that she'd catch one. It might be too dark for the rose to thrive, but I figured she'd do her best. The other I've planted in a pot so I can take it with me to grow new memories when I have to move.

~ *Cracks* ~

*…and under the pavement the soil
is dreaming of grass.*

(Wendell Berry)

The old yard is an emptiness of grey – a tennis-court sized base with a side of pitted concrete and a bleached wood wall. An empty farmyard is a strange, hushed place; it holds an air of waiting for something-to-happen about it. Once full of noise, it now seems devoid of life. No tractors or trailers rattle through; the cattle and sheep are silent. But if you look beyond the cracks, the rusted metal and broken gates, different lives can be found.

Cross to the old stone cattle feeder. It only took a week to fill with stair-rods of Welsh mountain-and-sea rain and it wasn't long before life appeared. Water boatmen scull with feather-fine fingers to the surface and hang upside down to draw breath before descending, clasping mercury-bubbles of air. Whirligig beetles like shiny-black rice grains twirl madly in circles, looking skyward with one pair of eyes and waterward with the other. Perhaps that's why they appear so frenzied – they're not sure which field of vision to follow.

Green algae called blanket weed forms when the sun is high, and the name describes it perfectly as it's capable of covering the water in a couple of days. I pull out soft emerald-green handfuls which I drape over the rough side of the trough so any pond-life can wriggle back into the water. Blanket weed is surprisingly silky to touch whilst in the water, but clings to your fingers when exposed to the air. The almost seaweed drying smell lingers for days. I leave a small patch in one corner as it gives the honeybees a safe surface to drink from.

Sparrows congregate on the crumbling wall behind, chattering, nudging, squabbling and jostling like children at the lido, arguing whose turn is it to go first. They fly down to drink and to take an occasional bath when the algae is strong enough to hold them. Sparrows normally like to nest near each other and have colonised an old shed and the hawthorn that is helping to hold it up, but a pair have gone up-market and are nesting in an old metal gantry attached to the wall, their slate grey and chestnut heads perfectly matching the rusting metal. Disembodied cheeps echo at feeding time.

The concrete isn't as flat as it appears to be. There's a slight tilt to the east so excess water can drain into the ditch, and decades of passing machinery have caused it to buckle and crack. Now these cracks are evolving, the winter deluge bringing soil and seeds which have started to colonise wherever they can. Cocksfoot and perennial rye grass are the first to appear, along with nettles and docks, which handily sit side-by-side, so you can rub with one after you get stung by the other. This year, there's a handful of foxgloves not yet flowering – they'll take another year before they do – and white clover, bittercress and groundsel weave between their feet. Buttercup-yellow dandelion and daisies, pink flushed by the sun, add a splash of colour, whilst in a shady corner, herb-robert reaches out, looking for the light. In autumn, the plant turns glorious shades of amber, copper and scarlet, and in summer its small pink flowers clash against the red of the stems, which have an unpleasant, almost burnt smell when picked, the reason why Stinky Bob is one of its country names.

There's a patch of blues under the self-sown sycamore (which I ought to pull out as it's beginning to crack the concrete even more) which I couldn't have orchestrated better myself. Speedwell, forget-me-nots and a stray violet inter-mingle with the little dangling, triangular heads of shepherds' purse. Germander speedwell has a tiny white eye and four petals, which are the same shade as the bluebells that wander through the wood nearby and its cousin, the common speedwell, is a shade darker. Both were used as good luck charms, sometimes being sewn into coat pockets, to 'speed you on your way.' Forget-me-nots are more turquoise and have five petals with a yellow-bead eye. This eye turns white when the flower has been pollinated, so the insects know there is no more nectar to be had. Their name is borrowed from the German, *Vergissmeinnicht*, which always reminds me of a war poem I read at school with that title. The flowers signify remembrance and have been chosen to represent the Alzheimer's Society, for obvious reasons. The two plants twine so tightly together, you can't tell where one ends and the other begins.

In the hairline fissures, a pea-green moss-like mat of procumbent pearlwort stretches in all directions, trying to find another gap to reach in to. The plant is almost unnoticeable as you walk across the yard as it sprawls horizontally, and you have to kneel to see it properly. The stems are smooth and succulent-like and the flower buds are like tiny baubles which open to chalk-white flowers which smell of nothing in particular. It's a tenacious little plant and seems to be able to grow anywhere including vertical walls, withstanding people, dogs and cars treading over it, and can apparently be submerged in water for a number of days with no ill-effects. It is said to be the first plant that Jesus set his foot on when he rose from the dead, and in Scotland, a spray on the door is said to keep the fairies away.

To many, the crumbling walls, exposed breeze blocks and cracked concrete are something that needs sorting, clearing, removing. But nature is slowly winning. She is creeping with green and brown fingers, poking into corners and smoothing rough edges. Rewilding speaks to me of doing something to actively encourage nature in all its forms. I have no hand in this – here, she is managing by herself.

~ *Fields* ~

'Without fields – no us.
Without us – no fields'
(Tim Dee)

What is a field? And when is a field a field and not a pasture? An area of open land typically bounded by hedges or fences, normally used for growing crops or for keeping animals, is one definition, pasture being land kept just for grazing. Fields are generally man-made and man-kept, otherwise they would return to scrub and woodland.

When we looked at places to move to, the main thing Dave wanted was fields – productive, boundaried, well-drained – suitable for farming sheep and growing hay. The house was a secondary consideration. That could be built, mended, adapted. Land was different. They're not making any more of it, he used to say. And if there were a few trees around or a small wood, even better.

Penbanc had all of those things. The land had 'good heart'; estate agent speak for fertile fields; deep hedges of hawthorn and blackthorn; an ancient woodland containing oak, ash, sycamore, birch, bluebell and primrose; a ravine with a stream at the bottom, trees clinging tightly to the sides; the occasional glimpse of sea on a clear day; red kite, buzzard, yellowhammer. It was very different from the subtle beauty of the marshland we'd left – waving reeds and grass criss-crossed with ditches and scrubby shrubs; reed buntings, barn owls, and snipe; geese in winter and skylarks in summer; water hawthorn and fen raft spiders.

It was all Dave had ever wanted. It wasn't until after he died that I got to know the fields as well as he did, especially as during lockdown, I couldn't go anywhere else. I knew the woods, the lane to the top of the drive, my garden, but the fields had always been full of sheep, grass waiting to be cut, or boundaries needing to be fenced, so my knowledge was limited. I sold the sheep and let the grass grow, getting a neighbour to cut it for hay and silage once a year only rather than the two or three cuts that was usual – I didn't need or want to fertilise the ground in any way. The hedges grew upwards and outwards, apart from the ones bordering the track towards the house, which I had to cut as I risked being enclosed by an impenetrable barrier of blackthorn, hawthorn and hazel, just like Sleeping Beauty.

It was then I began to know each field, know their similarities and differences; which parts lay wet for longer after the rain; how the elder blossom would appear a week later on the north side of the hedges; which blackthorn tree was best for picking sloes. How, just like the woods, every field had its own characteristics even though the geography, trees and plants were similar.

The field names were fascinating too. We'd been told the English translations of them when we first moved in, and later found a map with these names of them in Welsh. The original sound much more poetic – Cartws; Gwair; Penrallt; Main; Cromlech Uchaf and Isaf; Parc Di; Parc Dan; Penrhew; Parc y shed; Parc y Peg; Cwm.

It wasn't until recently that I found out that even these names may not be correct – the Welsh tithe maps say otherwise. Parc Cartws becomes Parky Fotlas and Parc bach; Gwair, Parc las; Parc Di, Cefn Bach; Parc Dan, Yr Allt; Park y Shed, Parc y Lon; Penrallt, Parc y Pant. The new cwm was divided into Parc Alban, Foxhole, Allt Foxhole and Waun Issa, the old Cwm into Parc y Cwm and Yr Allt. Only cromlech remained the same. As a lot of the hedges had been removed, there were more original names. Finding out what they all meant was another matter.

~ *Fields of Gold* ~

Parc Gwair (Hay field)
Mid-morning, early July

The landlocked sea of seeding grass is waiting to be cut. Wave upon wave of soft pink, beige and bronze sprinkled with the yellow shine of dancing field buttercups ripple and flow across the slope, only ceasing when they hit the dark green boundary of a hawthorn hedge. Under a sky the colour of a newly shorn sheep, a sweet and earthy, slightly sickly smell of a sun-kissed meadow permeates the air and it feels muggy and close. It's typical fly weather.

Growing in the hard-baked soil either side of the gateway, an underlay of low growing pineapple weed softens my footsteps. The plant seems to like the area around gateways and paths so it must like being trodden on. The small yellow with-a-hint-of-green petal-less flower heads are acorn shaped and when its feathery leaves are rubbed, they do smell of a ripe pineapple. They are apparently a good insect repellent, and you can make a pineapple crush flavoured tea from the flowers. Higher above the bank and under the sweep of collapsing grasses, dark green rosettes of primrose leaves nestle close to the ground. In spring, their pale-yellow flowers gleam in the shade created by the sycamore tree. They like being at the top of ground that slopes slightly, as even though they like moist soil, they don't want their feet wet all of the time.

I walk widdershins around the perimeter of the field. The hedgeline to the north consists mainly of gorse and was once straggly and sparse, but since severe pruning several years ago, it's become a tight knit, prickly barrier, with a few scrapes of bare earth at its feet where the sheep take shelter. The bushes seem to be almost permanently in flower, a fluorescent, eye blinding yellow in full sunshine. On such days, the smell of coconuts from the gorse flowers permeates this side of the meadow, but on this hazy day, the flowers are sulking tight. A few honeybees are trying in vain to gain entry but without success and a fluffy, amber-tinted common carder bee meanders to the pink of a blackberry flower instead. The gorse flower has a clever mechanism to ensure pollination. The first bee to land on a newly opened bloom triggers a spring so the bee is dusted with pollen and at the same time, the style touches the bee's stomach and picks up any pollen from the bee's previous foray.

Gorse, also known as furze, or *eithin* in Welsh, is a member of the pea family and is a pioneer plant, which means it can colonise poor soils by fixing nitrogen from the atmosphere via its roots. Historically, it was considered a useful plant, as it provided fuel for bread ovens, fodder for livestock, and when the branches are tied, as a brush for floors and chimneys. In Celtic mythology, gorse was burnt at Beltane because of its flammability and is considered to represent the sun and the god Lugh – the Celtic god of the sun and summer – and is believed to offer protection and optimism.

When dry, the seed pods of the gorse are long and black and dusted with white hairs. On a sunny afternoon, you can hear them pop as they twist and crack open, dispersing their seeds up to three metres away. There are pockets of gorse all over the farm, mainly where the ground is rocky and soil is thinnest and the plant can spread quickly if not controlled, being able to cover a field if not managed by man or beast. It's forever on the march in search of sunlight…

I run my hand along the top of the wave of grasses. They feel soft as feathers and tickle my palm. Holding one stem just below where the biscuit-coloured seed heads begin, I pinch it between thumb and index finger and pull up all the ripe seeds as I go, slowly letting them drip through my fingers onto the sward. Hopefully some seeds will germinate, leaving a memory of myself amongst the new growth.

The names of the grasses read like words from poetry. Sweet vernal, timothy grass, crested dogs' tail, sheep's fescue, creeping bent, perennial rye, Yorkshire fog, false oat. Mounds upon mounds upon mounds. After a heavy dew, they hold so much moisture, it's almost as if it's been raining, my jeans becoming soaked to mid-thigh, the denim dotted with the embroidery knots of tiny seed pellets.

Grass is an incredible plant. You can cut it, flood it, freeze it, dry it, and it nearly always grows back, even when it has been cut with a barber's number one in house-proud suburban gardens. Varieties of grass are probably the most important economically important plant family in the world. We use it for food, clothing, animal feed, insulation, biofuel, baskets, paper, thatching, to prevent soil erosion, as a surface for sport. And for making hay.

The weather has to be just right to make good hay. Three days of dry weather is ideal – one to cut, one for tedding (turning), one for raking and baling. It can be very technical if you're so inclined. The moisture content of the fallen grass is measured – it should be less than 20 percent before baling– but for small scale farming such as here, it's cut, dried and baled when there's a window of dry weather. An uncommon event in West Wales. We used to make silage – cut grass wrapped within 24 hours, so the grass becomes pickled and is easier for the sheep to digest – which is not so weather dependent, but this year a neighbour is cutting it for hay as I have no sheep to feed it to.

I've placed a bench at the top left-hand corner of the field and positioned it so you can see a sliver of the sea on a clear day if you sit and stretch your neck as tall as you can. Looking east and south, the fields and hedges of Penbanc stretch outwards, and meet up with those of my neighbours – nature knows no boundaries. The cloud stretches across the whole of the sky with no break of colour, making the sky feel nearer somehow. The only blot on the horizon, literally and metaphorically, is the quarry opposite, which has just had permission to expand. A once green field is now a gash of terracotta as they've removed all the topsoil. I can sometimes ignore the visual aspect of the quarry, concentrating instead on the stands of sycamore and ash that block it out if I get my angle of vision right, but it's the sound that irritates after a while. Not the distant noise of machines, as contrary to popular belief, the countryside isn't quiet all of the time. There's always the sound of a tractor, a chainsaw or an unrecognisable machinery noise somewhere, as well as the calls of sheep, cattle and cockerels and the occasional crack from a shotgun. It's the insidious, piercing, metronomic beep…beep…beep… of the diggers reversing, that gets on your nerves.

It's silent so far today. The only thing I can hear is the whisper of the grasses and the rustle of sycamore leaves; the pink of a chaffinch; a distant coo from the pigeons in the dutch barn; a male blackbird alarming. Overhead, a plane cruises to America. A solitary herring gull the same colour as the sky floats seawards towards Ceibwr Bay, and brown butterflies – ringlet, meadow brown, gatekeeper – lilt and weave their way through the vegetation in search of nectar or a mate. When they're all together, it's hard to tell them apart, it's only when they still and rest upon a leaf or a flower that I can tell the difference. The ringlet is dark and velvety, the colour of hot chocolate without any milk, and has barely visible eye spots; the meadow brown is nutmeg brown with two eye spots, and is slightly larger, whilst the gatekeeper has warm orange wing patches bordered with chestnut and has two highlights within each eye spot, which look like flashes when the wings open and close.

In the centre of the field is a shed where the pump and filter for the spring water is situated, exactly where the spiritual diviner said the well would be. There's a fence surrounding it so no animals can get in. Dave planted three apple trees, a pear and plum tree in the space. The pear refused to put up with the rain, wind and damp and succumbed after one year, but the others are growing, slowly. The red-over-gold, egg shaped fruit from the Victoria plum is loved by the wasps so it's a fight to see who gets to enjoy its sticky sweetness first, and one apple tree has so far failed to produce any fruit, but I like my mini-orchard. It's good for the insects and birds, if nothing else.

Tiny insects rise up from the ground as I winnow through the grasses and behind me, I see the grass-trodden evidence of where I've walked. The red, cream and shimmer-blue flash of a swallow skims past, forked tail streaming, a bird which looks like it flies just for the pleasure of it. It twists, rises, then scoops low, attracted by the insects disturbed by my feet. A second one joins the first, then a third, and they bank and turn and dive, searching for food, twittering and chattering all the while. Two more are perched on the telegraph wire, waiting to join the chase or to be fed. I once counted over 100 birds gathered on the same wire as they readied themselves for migration, and ten years ago we had 15 pairs nesting in the old barns. Even though the barns have stayed the same, I've made wallows when the ground is dry and never use any chemicals on the land, the number of pairs has got less every year. This year, there's only five, and I don't know what else I can do to change that. Some things are beyond my control.

~ *How Far Can a Ladybird Fly?* ~

It's the end of July and today the lane doesn't look like my lane. Later than usual, the council have carried out their annual beheading of all things green and beautiful and it's heart-breaking. I'd hoped they wouldn't come this year. I understand the long grasses that hide the corner of the road have to be managed for safety reasons, but there's no need for everything to be sacrificed in the name of visibility or red tape. Yesterday, the lane was a place of life – foxglove, yarrow, field buttercup, speedwell, red campion, birds foot trefoil, herb Robert, white clover, held together with twines of purple-pink field vetch and cleavers, and was a refuge for goldfinches, robins, skylarks, blackbirds, whitethroats, dunnock, yellowhammers. Spiders spun near-invisible homes and snails carried their own through the coolness of the collapsing plants.

Now all I can see is a desert of brown; naked stems broken. It's quiet too, almost as if the lane is in shock. No goldfinches peeping from their favourite hedge. No sign of the robin that sits in the same sycamore tree every morning. No iridescent trail of slug or snail. No butterflies, not even a bee. The summer smell of drying grass has been replaced by a dank smell of over-ripe fruit. Even the hard greyness of the road is hushed – thousands of seedheads and leaves and flower-tops soften my footsteps and this potpourri of dying vegetation is surprisingly slippery. When I get home, I'll find hundreds of seeds wedged between the furrows of my walking boots.

A dunnock stands a little further down, the colour of dead grasses and exposed earth. Its normal behaviour is to lurk in the tangle of undergrowth, so I imagine it must feel exposed in this newly barren landscape. It flies up into the hawthorn and gives a forlorn peep, different from its normal silvery warble. Further along, there's one remaining foxglove besides the gate, colours fading now but still bright against the brown. Hopefully, the plant will remain upright without collapsing, so its apple-green seedheads are able to ripen and fall. Each plant can contain a million seeds, which should be enough to enable at least one plant to grow from the harvest.

Then, on the bend looking seawards, and where the bank is over-my-head high, I spot a small cluster of harebells, these ones clever enough to miss the flail. With nothing apart from a stray curl of honeysuckle surrounding them, their colours are vivid against the now uniform brownness. These exquisite bells of mauve-blue, with a dab of white on the inside, flare at the edges, and sway with the gentlest of touches, dangling from a delicate swan-neck stem. Harebells are ephemeral beings and it's easy to understand why folklore tells us that they help transform witches to hares, and that their bells ring to signal a fairy gathering or to warn rabbits that foxes are nearby. There is a superstition that to hear harebells ringing was an ill omen. I wonder if they rang last night before the cutters arrived.

No grasses, no flowers. I wonder and worry about the insects, even those that sting and bite. How many were killed? Where do they lay their eggs? Where do they go to now to find food? How far does a ladybird have to fly before it finds a supply of aphids? How far can one fly?

(A ladybird travels up to 37 mph and its wings beat 85 times a second. They can remain in the air for up to two hours, which means they can potentially fly up to 74 miles with wind assistance, although it's more likely to be two.)

~ Night ~

The sun has flashed a farewell, the greyline fading as I make my way outside. The house is stifling on this July evening, my anxiety about leaving the farm making me breathless and longing for the outside air. I lean my hands against the waist high wall until my breathing settles and I'm becalmed. Blackbirds are evening-calling, as are the robin, dunnock, song thrush, and their familiar talk sooths and settles. Heavenwards, the colours are beginning to leach from the surroundings, the woods fading into inky blackness, the line of the horizon merging with the sky. Now I'm outside, I decide to stay here, to wait and see who and what owns this place when I'm usually sitting inside.

The pipistrelle bats have been zip-wiring since sundown. They roost in the farmhouse roof and in the cottage, streaming out of an invisible gap above the bathroom window, and I always count one hundred of them before stopping. I like that other creatures think of Penbanc as home, the bats, the sparrows that nest under the roof, even the very large spider that sits in the corner of the inglenook fireplace, which glares at me every time I come near.

Pipistrelles are the same weight as a twenty pence coin but are surprisingly noisy – I can hear them above my head at night, high pitched chattering, squeaks and shuffles in the attic space. They are more silent out here in the open, as the echo-location noise that helps them find food is above the threshold of my hearing. They quickly dodge, circle, swoop, to catch the gnats, flies and moths they feed upon and can eat up to 3000 insects a night. The only downside of sharing a home with bats is the amount of droppings they produce as I have to sweep the wall and floor outside the window every day. Bat droppings seem to stick to things.

I found a dead baby bat once when I went to sweep, a tiny thing, a pup. It had very little fur and was an all over grey-brown colour, unlike the more golden-brown colour of an adult. Pups live on their mothers' backs and feed on their milk until they can fly at around three to six weeks. I've also encountered bats inside my bedroom, crazily circling endlessly and knocking into things. The only thing to do is to leave all the windows open, shut the door and turn the light off, and hope they will find their own way out.

A strange thing happened this time last year. It was dusk, prime bat exit time, and I was sitting inside with the window open, when out of the corner of my eye, I became aware of a bird flying low in the enclosed garden. It disappeared, then circled again. I went upstairs to take a closer look and realised it was a juvenile sparrowhawk. There had been one in the garden a few days previously, trying and failing to catch birds near the bird table. This time, it was trying to catch the bats that were pouring out under the roof. Round and around it went, trying to catch the bats as they exited the house. This went on for over fifteen minutes, but I couldn't tell if the sparrowhawk managed to catch anything.

I hadn't been aware that bat catching was a sparrowhawk thing.

As the dark mantles, the patch of moon daisies I grew from seed glow from their position in front of the border and the quartered cream flowers of the climbing rose, *rosa sombreuil*, appear stuck against the wall as if by magic, their violet smell more pronounced in this half-light, the smaller tubular star flowers of jasmine winding through them. Paler flowers attract the moths and insects the bats feed upon, and these plants also need them for pollination, so I've planted different varieties of plants for that purpose all around the house. Sweet rocket and night scented stock, both in shades of white through to lilac, smell of almond with a hint of spice, whilst the tall spires of evening primrose with bowl shaped lemon-yellow flowers that have an edgy sweetness about them, open at night and have seeded themselves throughout the garden. They are faintly phosphorescent in this half-light and have a bright nectar guide pattern for moths and bats, which is invisible in daylight but present under ultraviolet light. Evening primrose seeds have high levels of gamma-linoleic acid, an omega-6 fatty acid, which is used in skin care, and the oil is taken as a supplement to aid premenstrual syndrome, menopause, arthritis and eczema.

An almost full moon has emerged, ushering in the dark. Everything looks, smells and feels different as soon as the night falls. Even the soundscape of the place has changed, making things seem nearer than they are, like the stream in the valley. Unless you stand alongside, the water trickles silently in the light of day, but in this indigo evening it feels only a few feet away. The smell of the flowers is stronger now and carries further, attracting all things that fly.

When it's dark here it's really dark. The first time I went outside on a clear evening when we moved here, I gasped at the brilliance of the stars. And there seemed more of them here on this Pembrokeshire night compared to a Sussex sky. Later, I'd stood in the middle of the path opposite the house and slowly rotated in a circle, arms wide, trying to absorb the beauty, the vastness of the night sky. I could only recognise a few stars and planets but resolved to learn more. The Plough lay opposite the back door, which meant I was facing vaguely north, whilst Orion, the hunter, carrying his shield in his right hand and his sword in his left, was running above the sycamore tree across the south-west, chasing the Pleiades, the seven sisters he fell in love with. Seeing Orion meant the return of colder weather, of winter.

Orion is not visible on this July evening as he disappears from this sky during the summer months. Instead, Sirius, the dog star rises – it's the brightest star in the sky. This leads to this time of the year being called the Dog Days of Summer, normally lasting from July third to August eleventh, a time which usually coincides with the beginning of the summer's heat. In *The Iliad*, Homer refers to Sirius as Orion's dog rising, and both Ancient Greeks and Romans associated the rising of the star with increased heat, disaster and fever.

I walk over to the only level area of concrete and sit down, the old wooden patio chair creaking as I lower myself into it – I don't normally notice the sound in the daylight. A waft of honeysuckle settles. Tiny flying creatures circle around my head, some brushing against my cheek, bright motes shining in the arc of light, and two moths spiral. Bats swoop low and circle, catching and eating, catching and eating.

I'm not as good at recognising moths as I am butterflies. Earlier this month, I accidentally left the porch light on and the next morning, the glass of the window was garlanded with moths of all different colours and sizes. Their names are things of beauty, like the moths they represent – green oak tortrix; ruby tiger; common footman; large emerald; pebble hook-tip; white ermine. Between the glass and the window frame a pale emerald moth nestled. A pale, almost translucent jade, with a pencil line of cream and darker jade threading from fore to hind wing, it is ethereally beautiful. The larvae feed on birch, hawthorn and oak. Nearby, the brimstone moth shimmers on the rough render of the wall. When resting, its wings form an angular heart shape of a bright yellow with wing notches of chestnut brown. On the forewings, two eyes of silver-blue flash. As I study the moths with intent, one flies from its resting place on the window and lands on my index finger. It's small, about a centimetre, and an unusual peach-pink colour, with black childlike squiggles drawn on the wings with a fine nibbed pen, and has long, curved antlers of pale buff. This moth is a rosy footman and the larvae feed on lichen that grow on oak trees.

In the nearly full moon glow, all colours drain from everyday objects, making them seem almost unrecognisable. Everything is a shade of grey, white or black. The chair sitting at right angles to the old railway carriage, its back stretched and tall, and a twin to the one I'm sitting on, has a regal air, like the poor relation of an Eisteddfod throne. The carriage looms alongside the blackened hedge, and only I know that it's held together by rusting corrugated iron sheets, invisible baler twine, crumbling mortar and tendrils of ivy, some as thick as my wrist. Ivy represents protection, healing, fidelity and, to the Druids, peace, because of its ability to bind different things together.

It takes a while for my eyes to adapt to the low light level, normally about ten minutes to notice a difference. A faint sweep of light crosses the fields in front of me then disappears, then again, briefly illuminating the hedgeline, the pumphouse, the sycamore, bathing everything in a silver wash. It's the beam from the lighthouse at Strumble Head, 21 miles away by road and is not visible every night – it must depend on the clarity of the air. The first time I saw the searchlight, I had no idea what it was, having little idea of the geography of this new place. The lighthouse lies due west from the kitchen side of the house, and on the map, it looks obvious, but it took a neighbour to explain, eventually. The lighthouse was built in 1908 to guide the way for ships travelling between Ireland and Fishguard harbour and is situated not far from where French soldiers landed in 1797, the last attempted invasion on the mainland of Britain.

I spot a dark shape not quite the size of a rugby ball moving slowly under the cherry tree. It's a hedgehog, snuffling, scratching, and it's searching for fallen peanuts under the bird feeder. Hedgehogs make a variety of sounds, grunting, huffing, hissing and they can be surprisingly noisy for small creatures. This one stops briefly by the bowl of water nearby, then trundles off into the tangled undergrowth below holly, hazel and rose.

A louder animal is the badger, or *mochyn daear*, which I look for and occasionally see in the half-light. I'd never seen one in the wild before I moved here. These unmistakable black and white brocks are the biggest land animals in Wales, weighing between 10-12 kg. There is a sett in the bottom fields, but badgers are seen all around here so I'm not sure if the ones I see are from there. Alongside their sett, which can be lived in for generations, the badger has a latrine area – badgers like to keep their homes clean. A few years ago, the Welsh government carried out a year of vaccination against tuberculosis in badgers, which for some reason they didn't continue. The men live-captured them by using peanuts, which badgers love, apparently. Badgers mainly eat worms, and have a favourite worm called *Lumbricus Terrestris*, the common earthworm or Night crawler. In some mornings, I can see visible evidence of their digging for worms in the fields, as snout-shaped holes litter the ground. Badgers also eat hedgehogs. Nature can be cruel, but not as cruel as humans can be.

The common toad, *Bufo bufo*, abounds here. I know they're ambling around, searching for food, as I occasionally disturb them whilst gardening. They like to eat slugs and snails and apparently the larger ones can also manage a slow worm, if lucky enough to find one. I've only seen one slow worm here, and that one had its head bitten off. Toads lurk under plant pots, compost heaps, in shallow scrapes in the soil and hibernate in the winter. They come together in swarms to mate in breeding ponds in February. It's estimated that two tonnes of toads are killed on roads every year as they migrate to their breeding grounds.

I've found their spawn in the water trough in Quarry field, and it's recognisable from frog spawn by being laid in strings rather than in rounds. The tadpoles are matt black, whilst frog tadpoles are specked with gold, and they take between two and three months to metamorphose into toads. Their secretive nature, poison secreting skin and warty appearance of these amphibians mean that myths and legends swirl around them. The devil was reputed to masquerade as a toad; witches used them as familiars so you had to remove one carefully if found in a room; in nearby Nevern, a man called Longshanks was eaten by a plague of toads, even though his friends pulled him into a tree in a bag to escape; and in Welsh mythology, the Water Leaper, or *Llamhigyn Y Dwr*, which ate fish as well as the fishermen that caught them, is described as a giant toad with bats wings, no back legs and a long tail with a sting at the end.

I shift on the chair as the air becomes cooler and the faint breeze fades. The bats and moths that had been circling are no longer visible. It's so quiet that the air feels heavy, as if it's pressing down somehow. One of the dogs barks inside the house, loud through the silence. Time to go into the warmth of the house. I felt scared at night sometimes, living here by myself at the end of the lane. Never with the moon animals, the birds, the insects, which make the night their own, journeying when the sun creatures were asleep. Not even with the ghosts, the spirits who are forever tied to this place. No, it was humans I feared, people that might come down the lane by design or by chance. The poachers, the badger boys, the snarers, or worse. Once, a van turned up unexpectedly when the light was fading. I happened to be outside, just returning from locking away the chickens and luckily had the dogs with me, which may have been the reason why the van turned and went back the way it came. It was enough to keep me permanently on edge. The creatures of the night however, carried on their ways regardless.

~ *Perambulating* ~
(A slow walk round a place especially for pleasure)

Three Quarries, Three Houses.

The month of August is a muted month. All things feathered quietened and hushed, all things green, soft around their edges. As if nature is taking a breather from the green busyness of spring and early summer. It's a time to relax. This August however, I'm feeling ungrounded rather than relaxed as the farm has been sold. A mixed blessing, more so as I haven't found somewhere to move to. Since then, I've been wanting to walk around each field every day, as if to fix memories of this place deep within – maybe this will help ground me. I do cheat sometimes and use the quadbike, but the urge to walk slow is ever present.

I read somewhere about the custom of beating the bounds, or perambulating the bounds. Every seven years, prominent citizens of a town would walk the boundaries of the parish with a group of boys, who would beat the so-called boundary stones with willow or hazel wands so they would remember where the stones were. The boys would sometimes be knocked against the stones as well, to 'aid' their memory, so they could pass the knowledge of these boundaries on, parish boundaries being important for both historical and financial reasons.

I'm not sure if my longing is anything to do with that custom, to know, to feel where everything is and where everyone's boundary lies, but seeing where the houses are rooted from seems important. Rather than rushing from one place to the next, there is this need to walk, to perambulate, to take time around each quarry. And due to lockdown, there's plenty of time. And although I have no knowledge that each house is built from stone from each quarry, there are three quarries here and three houses.

I've always felt a connection to quarries, especially ones no longer in use. They seem places between places, liminal spaces between the air and deep earth, crossover places with a landscape all of their own. There's both visual and tactile evidence of time through the ages all around. Many of my forbears were quarrymen, blasting out rock and dying from dust in their lungs, one travelling across the sea to fight a war in a foreign land, to tunnel, to blast, to dig. My grandfather built dry stone walls with remnants picked up from the quarry floor and scoured the same rocky surface every morning looking for sheep that may have fallen from the top. I'm named after the place where one of these quarries is situated, Vaynor near Merthyr Tydfil, a limestone quarry used for lime needed in the production of iron for Crawshay's Cyfartha ironworks. My school house name was Quarry.

Quarry field (Parc Main). Day one.

Today, the sky is more white than blue, and the wind stops and starts in a half-hearted attempt to blow a few fallen leaves around. They drift in circles around the edge of the path, not really going anywhere. The sun, a watery version of itself, flickers through the sycamore tree but is too weak to cast a shadow, a change from the heat of the last few days. The long grasses on each side of the lane are bleached-blond and starting to collapse. It's the end of summer and everything is beginning to fade at the edges.

I walk up the lane past the farmhouse and on the left is a new agricultural barn, full of things that had been left behind or things we'd brought with us and still haven't used. It's unlikely I'm going to need any of them now. At the back of the building lies a ladder leading to a makeshift den the children who lived here before had made, the edges of planks and pallets now disguised by strands of ivy sneaking through the broken window at the back of the barn. The den provides an occasional roost for a barn owl which I've rarely seen but know it's been there because of the small mounds of pellets lying on the floor underneath, now grey and crumbling into bone saturated dust.

In front of the barn is a flat, gravelled area where the beehives are situated. Someone else comes to take care of them and I am rewarded with a pot of honey per hive.

Driving down the drive last summer, I saw the beginning of a bee swarm and stopped to watch. Swarms are basically a means to create a new colony – the old Queen leaves with half of the bees from the hive to search for a new home – but there is nothing basic about watching this event. The air above the hives was full of bees frantically flying this way and that with no discernible pattern to this frenzy, with more bees joining the throng and covering the whole of the air-space above the hives. Even through the shut window, the noise of them was incredible, a low pitched hum which thrummed through the air. Then as if by magic, they blended together into a tighter formation and moved southwards like a twister towards a low growing beech tree. I was surprised how quickly they settled, the queen finding a place to rest whilst the scout bees searched for a new home. Without intervention, the swarm might stay in the same position for a couple of days, but I rang the beekeeper to let him know, so he could move them into another hive if he wished.

I walked up later that evening to see how they were. The swarm hung from the tree and spread a short distance up the trunk. It looked like a piece of strange fruit, golden-brown and barely moving. The bees' hum had lessened, so you wouldn't know they were there.

The bees are quiet today, a few foraging among the surrounding plants, others flying further afield. A small copper butterfly is sunning itself on the barn wall. Its colour of teak with orange wings and frills matches the wood and the rust. Scattered amongst the few heads of red clover growing through the gravel are taller patches of cat's ear, with dandelion-like flowers, and common knapweed, thistle-like without thistles, its flowers of purple and pink beginning to seed. The tiny flowers of common sorrel, knobbly to the touch and strung like beads along hip-high stems, are changing from lime green to rose through to red. Brambles are advancing from the treeline and beginning to swamp a large pile of hardcore that had been left when the drive was re-laid. I'm not sure which looks most messy, but at least the brambles provide food for the wildlife. Along the margins are the usual sycamores and ash, plus a planted horse chestnut tree which flowered for the first-time last year.

A fat, black caterpillar covered in bristles ripples across the gravel, and I break off a dock leaf, laying it in front of the caterpillar to walk upon, not wanting to accidentally tread on it – there are few enough of them around. The caterpillar curls into the shape of a six or a nine depending on which way you look at it, and I gently scoop it onto the leaf and place it amongst the greenery.

One of the gateposts leading into Quarry field has dropped so the gate won't open. A tree with silvery, vertical striations helps prop it up on one side. The leaves are now a dark green instead of their spring lightness and have toothed edges with a tiny twist at the end. This shape and translucent greenness of the leaves in spring made me think it was a beech, but the leaves stayed on the tree during the winter which is characteristic of a hornbeam. Hornbeams have very hard wood so are also known as ironwood trees. This one is doing well as a gatepost, and I hold onto it as I climb over the gate.

I follow the sheep path around the edge of the top field which runs alongside the drive and realise that I always walk around the field the same way and do in every field. Maybe because the route is familiar and I like to notice what is changing from one day to the next, or maybe I'm just a creature of habit. Badgers and foxes also use the sheep path, plus the occasional rabbit. There aren't many rabbits here unfortunately. Maybe due to years of them being controlled, or maybe due to myxomatosis, a dreadful disease introduced in the 1950s that has decimated the rabbit population, initially having a 99.8 percent mortality rate. You can tell a 'myxy' rabbit easily. For a start, you can get near to one, as they go blind.

At the top of the field lies the shale quarry which gives the field its name. It's about 22 strides long and 15 wide, and one side is very steep – I don't go near the edge, especially as the shale fragments that dominate the area are slippery when you put your foot on them, plus I don't like heights. A large blackberry bush sits right in the centre of the quarry floor whilst a stand of gorse surrounds the bottom of the drop. The grass here is sparse and dry even in the winter, its usual greenness tinged with grey. It always feels warmer here, the rocks reflecting the sun, the hollow protected from the wind. A pocket of silver, pewter, yellow, olive-green, this area has its own micro-climate plus its own plants, birds and insects – common toadflax, creeping tormentil, silverweed; linnet, redpoll, wheatear, stonechat; yellowhammer; common blue butterfly, grasshopper,

I sit amongst the warmth at the bottom of the hollow, the stones and shale hard beneath my clothes and pick up a handful. Grey and smooth, angular and jagged, the shale varies in size from thumb size to feet size. Shale is a sedimentary rock, formed of compressed mud and silt, whilst slate is the same, but has been heated under pressure by the earth's crust so is harder. I think this is shale rather than slate because you can easily split the layers of rock by hand. The shale here wouldn't be strong enough to be used for roof tiles or for building, unless concreted together.

The smell of the quarry is different from the field, a mixture of metal, of dry, of closeness. A few small yellow flowers of the creeping tormentil meander through the grass and curl over the foot of the quarry whilst the taller toadflax stands bright against the dark of the gorse. The spikes of snapdragon-like flowers are primrose-yellow, with a dash of sunset at its throat. It's such a pretty flower but has a bitter, sour smell up close. A rush of small birds fly over the top of the quarry, tinkling and undulating – goldfinches come to feed on the seedheads of the grasses – and a seldom-seen chaffinch flies into the heart of the mound of gorse. There are so few of them around now, due to trichomonosis, a parasite which causes their throats to swell so they starve to death.

Behind me in the meadow, I can hear the call of a male grasshopper, similar to a quieter, daytime cicada, but although I'm lying at insect height, I can't see him.

The common grasshopper isn't as common as it used to be.

A crunch of hoof on rock, and my three pet sheep come to join me, nudging and pushing, one lowering his head for a rub, one nibbling on my pocket hoping for food. They're old boys now, eleven and twelve, but their teeth are intact, so they are still able to chew on grass. Roger, Freddy and Scruff, all named whilst running around the kitchen after being orphaned or ignored, warmed by the Raeburn and handfed for months. Sheep aren't as stupid as people think they are. They like to be in a herd as they are a prey animal and more numbers offer more protection; they can recognise up to 50 people; they can problem solve; they have an excellent sense of smell and can see almost 360 degrees due to their rectangular pupils without turning their head; they can choose specific plants to help them when they're ill, if available, of course; they are sociable animals and form close bonds with others. They are often blamed for the destruction of landscapes, but it was us that put them in such places. Sheep just have a bad press.

Standing, not wanting to be pushed over by them, I follow their footmarks to the top of the field and look across to the sea, today a thin, grey-blue hazy line merging with the sky, and over to the ridge of the Preseli hills, only visible on a clear day. Their edges are blurred so rain might be on its way. A pair of painted lady butterflies meander through the brambles. They look like faded tortoiseshells, with colours of copper, tan and black, dotted with white and have arrived here from North Africa. They flitter over the large round cement water trough that sits between this field and our neighbour's field – a crossing point, an open border. I've put a hurdle over half of it to stop his lambs from jumping into it. Three goldfish live here, won from a fair by the children of before. One is lying near the top of the water, dappled and cool under the trees, its fins only just moving. Toads have come to spawn here the last few years, so I've placed a large branch across the side to help the toadlets clamber out.

There's a slope downwards towards the stream line, and here, unseen by the road, is the worse evidence of past farming practises, the use of this hidden part of the field as a dump. Old oil tanks, corrugated iron sheets, tyres, barbed wire through old fenceposts, pram wheels, plastic buckets and worse. Too much of it and too dangerous to move. Thankfully, nature is helping to disguise this eyesore. Brambles, shrubs and a small tree growing up through the middle of it shows how long it's been there, festering.

So much of it is blocking the path, so I have to retrace my steps to approach from a different angle. This part of the field forms a long triangle where it meets the neighbour's land. A winter spring brings two fields together again – they both used to belong to Penbanc. This small, enclosed space seems separate from the rest of the field. The unpruned arms of the trees encircling the clearing trap the sparse sunshine and the light outlines tiny, flying creatures floating in the air. More gorse and bramble lie along the right side, plus hazel and what I thought was blackthorn on the left. But one October, on the forage for sloes to make sloe gin, I saw branches dripping with larger, deep purple fruit, three times the size of a sloe – the tree was more aubergine than green, its unpruned branches covered in a silvery green web of lichen, so full of fruit that some branches were touching the ground. These were damson trees, and further behind, bullaces.

Up close, the fruit is a smooth blue-purple with a white bloom. Whilst sloes are only one centimetre, damsons are two to three, bullaces in-between, although it's sometimes difficult to tell the difference just by looking. One way of distinguishing them is that blackthorn has long, deep spikes as thorns, whilst the damson has none, and although I'd happily eat a damson, no way would I eat a sloe. Damson jam is one of the best of jams, a deep, rich purpleness of flavour. However, picking out all of the kernels takes a while. So this year, I'm making jelly, not jam.

Jelly is a fiddle to make but there's a sense of measured time and timelessness about it. Everything done in the right order, nothing rushed. The drip, drip, drip of liquid through a jelly bag left overnight, then in the morning the kernels and skin left on one side of the bag and a beautiful purple liquid in a bowl on the other. As the sugar is added and stirred into the liquid, the colour darkens to a rich red-purple, and when poured into a jar and held up to the light, it's like looking through stained glass.

Little pots of sunlight and rain and trees.

There's a line of hazel trees on the way back to where I started, all growing on a bank a little higher than the field. They run in an almost straight line, so it looks as if they've been planted deliberately. All show signs of being coppiced, so they may have been. These coppiced branches stretch skywards and are upright and tall, and most are about twelve foot and above – they haven't been cut for a while. Dave cut a dozen or so a few years ago to use as pea sticks, so a few branches are shorter. I've brought a pruning saw with me as I want to make a thumb stick to use when walking, so choose a branch that's easy to get at – many are growing too close together – and cut a shoulder height length. The wood is grey and green and has a faint sheen when the light catches it and will need to dry and harden before I can use the branch as a stick. I'll strip off the bark in a spiral which will expose the darker wood underneath just to add a little decoration and angle the top so I can place my thumb on top of it whilst walking. I want the stick for when I'm perambulating in as yet unknown places away from the farm.

The wood and the glade with no name. Day two.

It's raining the next day, a soft, summer rain that wets you more than you think it will. There's a patter of water on leaf. Through the crown shyness of trees, the sky lies heavy and grey, the colour of a wood pigeon's wing.

At the bottom of quarry field and forming the border with the garden behind the farmhouse lies a wood and a glade with no name. The path running through it is the remains of the old green lane leading towards Cardigan which is now used as a flight path by the tawny owls that live here. The wood stretches northwards to become the tail of the larger woodland, whilst in the glade lies the second quarry at an almost throwing distance from the farmhouse and the cottage.

The cottage was once a cow shed, then a stable. One inside wall is made of stone similar to that in this quarry. The wall is of double height and just below the ceiling are a run of blocked up holes the size of the length of a brick. Apparently, they were once the nesting places of pigeons, who would lay eggs and raise their chicks, until the young, known as squabs, were big enough to eat but as yet unable to fly, so they could be caught easily. A source of readily available, cheap meat.

The glade has a background of trees on one side – ash, sycamore, hazel – and the bottom of the quarry on the other. The quarry is the height of a small tree and I take 15 strides to walk from one side of the glade to the other. It is quite different to the other one, a place of shade rather than sun. In early spring, the floor is covered with snowdrops, which spread in a white mist down the slope towards the stream. Bluebells follow, forcing their blue way through the early wands of bracken. I've planted some woodland daffodils here, also known as Lent lilies, or Peter's leek, *Cenhinen Pedr*, in Wales. They have a dark yellow trumpet and pale-yellow petals the colour of primroses and lie close, creeping and carpeting the woodland floor. As the year turns, the light soon becomes dark in a woodland, so no summer flowers grow here. Today, the wood is deep in a Stygian darkness, holding only memories of flowers.

The wood is home to greater spotted woodpeckers, nuthatches, coal and willow tits, as well as the owls. Bats fly between here and the house. Speckled wood, comma and holly blue butterflies cruise along the woodland ride. A garden warbler, taupe-brown and nondescript, but with a rich, melodious, rippling song, journeys between the woodland and the garden. I've twice seen the phantom of the forest, a goshawk, *Accipiter gentilis*, weaving expertly like a jet pilot through the trees in this part of the wood. They have similar colouring to a sparrowhawk, with a black-against-white barred chest and underside of wings, and a grey back. A female goshawk can reach the size of a buzzard. They are ambush predators, which means they can sit motionless until they launch an attack.

I stand in the middle of the glade, rain gentling down my face, the horizontal layers of rock and stone in shades of grey, brown and pale terracotta curving around me. A young ash tree, spindly and pale, pushes through one side of the quarry, dislodging blocks and dribbles of stone. Larger pieces of rock lie scattered about the floor, their hardness softened by a coat of moss and an elder tree is beginning its life amongst them. This area has always seemed like an otherworld, a secret, thin place, its hollowness emphasised by the moving arches of trees almost touching overhead; chapel-quiet below them. The slope behind stretches fieldward, the other streamward, and on the path linking the two, a stone statue of a woman, who I've named Blodeuwedd, stands in one corner, a frond of ivy winding and suckering around her waist and chest, reaching out a dark green leaf to touch her shoulder.

I've placed seven tree stumps in a circle close to the statue which I sit on whilst trying to think of nothing, and sometimes light a fire in the space created in-between the once-living seats, in order to honour certain dates, and to toast marshmallows. It's a place for such things.

I sit on one trunk now, ignoring the damp. The humus smell of dry earth after rain rises, especially strong after the days of heat. An overhead crow caws as it passes over and blue tits chatter from the depths of the trees. Most are of ash and sycamore and are tall and slender, most branches and leaves concentrated at the top. None have been thinned. They bend and sway easily in the wind, whispering and sighing. The leaves of all the trees are a similar colour now, a mid-green, unlike the varying colours of their new growth. They drip with lianas of ivy, which bind some of the trees together, and honeysuckle twists which are almost invisible but give away their presence by their evening smell.

Sitting still in the wood is something I've come to do, rather than walk the dogs in it all of the time. It calms and soothes. Sitting amongst trees is known to be beneficial. Forest bathing, a Japanese practice known as *shinrin-yoku*, was developed in the 1980s, although I'm sure that many have been doing it for longer, aware of the positive effect it could have on their mood. It also improves our immunity as the forest air is full of phytoncides, essential oils given off by trees. Apparently, twenty minutes a day is all we need to benefit from the bounty of the forest or wood – the smell of earth after rain; the sound of a nearby stream or the patter of rain on leaf; birdsong all around.

A spotted flycatcher, *Muscicapa striata*, rises up from the hazel near to me, then drops down onto the same branch, flicking its tail as it sits. It's the same size as a robin, but leaner, with a buff-brown back and paler chest, and is more streaked then spotted, the streaks running through its crown and upper breast. Always alert for food, it sits upright, ready to fly up and catch a passing insect, which it does with a snap. They are delightful to watch as they dart and twist and return and I watch it for a while before it flies to another perch. This flycatcher will be leaving for Africa soon and it's probably only been here a couple of months to breed. It's on the red list for conservation, 89 percent of the flycatcher population declining between 1967 and 2012.

Further along the enchanter's nightshade, *Circaea lutetiana*, borders the path. The plant is named after Circe, the Greek goddess of magic. Considering its name, it's an inconspicuous plant, having tiny white flowers with pink stamens on stems rising from heart shaped downy leaves. In the dappled shade of the woodland edge, however, where the green of the stems becomes at one with their green surroundings, these flowers look like they're floating in the air, as if by magic.

The path runs in front of three graves, those of our dogs, Rosie, Daisy and Roxy; one black Labrador who thought she was a sheepdog, and two Rottweilers, both as gentle as the rain. An elder tree umbrellas above them and I've fashioned a make-shift bench from two more tree stumps and part of an old scaffold plank so I can sit alongside and remember. Each grave has a piece of shale from the quarry engraved with each of their names.

The quarry in the Cwm. Day three.

Today is a day of sparkles and light – yesterday's raindrops holding the early morning sun; pools in the yard mirroring sky-blue and clouds; spiders webs in the hedges capturing sunbeams. The swallows are flying high; the sparrows splashing in the water trough. A pair of great tits chatter. There's a smell of wet concrete drying after rain.

The third quarry lies hidden in the cwm and the greenlane leading to it runs from the yard, through Parc y shed and Parc Penrhiw on one side, and Parc Dan and Parc Dai on the other, then through the woodland until it reaches the new Cwm. The greenlane is wider than most of the footpaths but not wide enough for a tractor. The last owners of Cwm, the house, used to drive a motorbike and sidecar along it, when the house was liveable.

A tumble of plants line the side of the upper lane – foxglove, red campion, herb robert, briar rose, self-heal, hawkbit, nipplewort, field buttercup, hedge bedstraw – whilst striated rock and thin grass form the base. The foxgloves are going over, their seed heads browning, and I shake a stem to help scatter any seeds. Walking downwards into the shade, the flowers are replaced by grasses – perennial rye grass, cocksfoot, common bent. A pair of blue tits chase across the lane, blue and yellow-bright, and on the path in front of me lies a buzzard feather, soft brown and cream, edges curled with yesterday's rain.

A fat horse fly lands on my bare arm and I shake it off before it can bite, but it comes back again and again until I manage to swat it. Only the females bite. They have serrated jaws that saw into skin and need blood for protein so they can produce eggs. Unlike mosquitos, they don't release any anaesthetic when they bite which is why the bite mark hurts so much. Males have weaker jaws and only feed on nectar and plant sap.

On a small piece of ground under an ash tree, a patch of climbing corydalis, *Ceratocapnos claviculata* is growing. It's a blink-and-you'll-miss-it sort of plant, with thin trails and tendrils of pale green stems and buttercream flowers and is scrambling across the nearby plants rather than climbing. It's apparently quite rare in that it's an indicator of an ancient woodland.

Dave laid the hedge along the Parc Penrhiw side. It's strongly growing now, the hazel and ash and blackthorn blended together so it's hard to tell where one ends and the other begins. The hedge is growing as he hoped it would – he never got to see what it was supposed to do. If maintained, the hedge will act like a fence but a living one and will keep the sheep where they are meant to be. Hedge-laying is an art and there are many styles depending on the geography, climate and types of trees growing, and what animals you want to contain. Dave learnt his technique in Sussex where the hedge is cut and layed over making a double brush, and the pleachers – the cut stems – are held using upright stakes. In the Welsh borders, the stakes are set at an angle, so rainwater can run down them rather than the stools (the base of the cut tree) so they won't rot, and dead wood is put into the hedge to stop the new growth being eaten by sheep.

A newly laid hedge is a beautiful thing.

Further down the lane, the hedge line becomes a tree line, some trees scrambling for a foothold on the top of banks, and the lane gradually becomes a holloway, a sunken lane, formed by erosion of feet, human and animal, and I imagine of water – in winter, the bottom of the holloway floods where it reaches the field.

My eyes are soon unable to see over the top of the bank and I keep walking downwards. The light lessens here with only the glimpses of sky through the gaps in the leaves and the opening at the end of the holloway. I turn to the right, to follow a footpath which leads to the deserted house, Cwm, and the quarry which lies next to it. The house is surrounded by trees and a small hazel is growing where the kitchen used to be. It has no roof – it was apparently deliberately removed. Dave, being a bricklayer in a previous life, said this house had been better constructed than the farmhouse. But now its chimney is broken and the walls are beginning to collapse inwards, some stones dropping into the quarry they originally came from. Armfuls of ivy are trying to do the job the mortar once would have done. The gap where the front door once hung leads into the kitchen, where an old oven still sits in situ in the wall, the door now rusted and pitted, alongside navelwort and a common spleenwort fern. There's still a mantelpiece above the fireplace. I wonder how many arms have leant against it, how many fires have been lit here. Cwm, the house that was once a home to many families, is now too dangerous to go into, so I leave it to the creatures that have made it theirs.

The quarry sits alongside the house but you'd hardly know it was there as it has fallen in on itself and is now smothered in bramble, ivy and bracken so I can't tell if it's another shale quarry or of stones. I'm presuming the latter as there's a small stone building in front of it, an outbuilding of some kind, built from various sizes of grey, white and crystal threaded rocks.

In spring, the floor of this area is covered with snowdrops, so many that you can't avoid stepping on them, and weeks later, primroses lighten the ground underneath the trees, yet to come into full leaf. Some aren't the usual pale-yellow colour, but a muted pink, I'm not sure if these are a mutation or the result of a bee foraging further afield. The primroses run all the way along the path on both sides – a primrose path.

Nearer to the walls that enclose the house, early purple orchids, *Orchis mascula*, push through the bare soil, with spires of rosy-purple rising from a rosette of green covered with dark purple blotches. The flowers don't produce nectar but attract bumble bees and other insects because of their colour and scent. Once the flowers have been fertilized, the plant apparently gives off a smell similar to a Tom cat's urine, but I've never wanted to get close enough to find out.

A huggable oak tree leans over the path, betwixt wood and field. Lammas shoots have emerged from the lower part of the trunk, lime green with rosy tips, and they stand out against the now uniform green of the older trees. These leaves are the trees' response to stress – lack of water or heat, or animal or insect activity, leading to defoliation of its spring leaves. They're called Lammas shoots as the emergence of them coincides with Lammas day, the first of August, or Lughnasadh, *Gwyl galan Awst*, which is the beginning of the first wheat harvest.

Against the brown of a tree, there's a slight movement and I turn to look more closely. A small bird, created in the colours of the earth, is mousing up the tree, merging with the bark. It's a treecreeper, *Certhia familiaris*. Treecreepers build their nest under a flap of bark and make it from moss, feathers and spiders' webs. A group of tree creepers is called a spiral, maybe because the bird spirals around the tree trunk. These birds can only travel upwards, not downwards, due to their long tail. If close enough, they have been known to do the same to people…

Beyond the footprint of Cwm lies Waun Issa, a wet, marshy area, mounded with soft rushes, and marsh marigolds in spring. It's littered with the fallen branches of many trees, some covered in moss and other things that live in damp places. The air lies still and hushed and speckles of light filter through the canopy of willow and alder. I've occasionally startled a woodcock here, a bird this environment is made for, as it ranges between the damp and the wood. Now rare, the woodcock, *Scolopax rusticola*, digs for worms and beetles in the soft earth with a long tapering bill. They are crepuscular birds, feeding mainly at dawn and dusk and when disturbed during the day, take off with a whirr and a zigzag of a flight. Like the treecreeper, it's a bird of its surroundings, of the earth and the trees, a swirl of russet and brown and fawn.

A huge beech tree stands guard over the entrance to this otherplace. There were once two, but one fell a few winters ago. It's still here, half in the water, and half out, a bridge between two worlds. The standing tree has the initials of the children of before carved into the bark and these have stretched and moulded with time. This triangular area marks the extent of our land. I still call it ours, although I suppose it's mine, temporarily, at least, and we've only borrowed it after all.

I leave Cwm and retrace the path to the hollowlane, turning right towards the fields, the new cwm. This one field consisted of two before the hedgerow was removed, I don't know how long ago; Parc Alban and Foxhole, which doesn't seem to have a Welsh name, according to the tithe maps.

Unlike the old cwm, which is the remains of an ancient meadow, this meadow has been re-seeded at one time. There's a sweep of a slope leading to a stream at the bottom end plus a scrubland at the top. Scrub always seems an inadequate name for this transitional place which provides such a benefit to nature, holding young trees, grasses and flowering plants and all of those species that thrive in such areas. Dave used to cut some of the scrub back so it didn't all revert to woodland, the scrub here being mainly blackthorn, hawthorn, hazel, gorse and sycamore.

Just off centre of Parc Alban lies a rocky outcrop, known as Arthur's seat to the family that lived here before us. Three twisted oaks, and a gnarled apple tree, their branches entwined and growing almost symbiotically with each other, frame a harsh, vertical outcrop of sandstone and shale, the lower stone gentled with moss. It resembles a throne constructed from rock and tree root. If you sit on its grey-cold surface under the awning of the trees and allow yourself to just be and listen to the silence, you can sometimes feel the energy changing. It becomes timeless in some way, in fact time ceases to matter. Another thin place in this place of ghosts and memories.

I sit there now and look around, the slate cool underneath. The uncut meadow ripples in waves of buff and beige from hedge to scrub and there's the smell of sun on grass. Birds call across the woods, vying with the distant low rumble from Trefegin quarry. A lone brown butterfly drifts across the peninsular of bramble. This place is quite beautiful, but there's a bittersweet quality about being here. Maybe there's too many memories today.

Around the corner of the throne lies a large stone that has been chiselled or hammered into a water trough, although you'd have to walk to the stream to fill it up. The sides are remarkably straight, the bottom flat and smooth. And cold – the water would have stayed cool for some time. Full of leaf litter, soil, acorns and sycamore keys when I first came across it, I brought back a spade to clear the hidden space, even though it didn't take long before it filled up again. Today, the trough is half full, but I won't clear anything now. I'll leave it for another to find.

There is no quarry in this field but there is another building in Foxhole which must have been built using stones from the one next to Cwm. We were told it was a shepherd's hut, but it seemed larger, well, the footprint of it was – there was no roof to be seen. Another lost place returning to the earth. A greenlane runs behind the hut, now overgrown as it hasn't been walked on for years. It leads on from the holloway I've just walked along and eventually leads to Parke, a near neighbour, and once this field belonged to that farm.

I walk back to the crossroads where the holloways and the bottom of Penrallt field meet. A wood warbler is singing, a call that starts quickly and then speeds up. I catch a glimpse of the bird sitting on the branch of an oak tree; a splash of a yellow-green and silver. It too will be returning to Africa soon. I follow its flight and look across to the quarry and Cwm, the house, both intertwined with the dark of the trees. The first day we looked around Penbanc, a red kite flew out of the ruined house, which I took as some sort of sign. I'm longing to see one today, but both sky and woods are silent.

~ *The Wonder of a Barn Owl* ~

> *...a pale face hovering in the*
> *afterdraught of the spirit, making*
> *both ends meet on a scream...*
>
> (R.S. Thomas)

Tawny owls live and breed in these woods. I hear them in the cool freshness of an early spring morning and when dusk mantles upon the trees; hear their answering calls when I'm lying in my bed with the windows open. The *tu-wit, tu-who* reminiscent of a fairy story. I've only seen them on a few occasions however – dark striations against a paler fluffed body, the size of a pigeon that's eaten the next-door farmer's corn. A silent soar from hazel to ash.

There's no evidence that barn owls breed here. The slippery, shininess of metal barns isn't conducive to a barn owl looking for a home. Even when we put up an owl box, none seemed interested. Only the aforementioned pigeons nested inside, and they seem to nest anywhere.

I've seen barn owls though, seen them appear almost magically, floating between barn and gate; cruising the hedges; a ghost-like tremble skimming the greyline. You'll never hear one approaching; they arrive with no warning – hovering, swooping and gliding silently, gently, resembling an oversized moth. They seem suspended in time and space, their wings almost too large for their small body. And they are almost weightless – a mature barn owl weighing less than a pound.

Barn owls are a macabre orchestra of otherworld sounds – screeching, screaming, shushing, hissing, which is why they used to be known as the demon owl. The call of an owl was once considered a bad omen and they were associated with death, especially as they were regularly seen around graveyards.

Following two days of snow, one roosted in the top barn. As I crunched my way up the drive early one morning, it appeared from under the lip of the roof, an almost touchable distance away from me and soared past me without a sound. Unlike the sheep, whose white fleece seems dirty when seen against the pristineness of snow, the underside and face of this owl were bright white. And somehow, the not-of-this-world silence of the bird's flight echoed the silence of the snow. Throughout the year, I found charcoal-grey owl pellets underneath the wooden beam, evidence the barn owl must have roosted there again, even though I rarely saw one.

A barn owl's talons are extremely sharp and it's likely that their prey is killed by a claw not a beak. One talon has a comb to groom their heart shaped facial disc, which is surrounded by tiny stiff feathers of tan and gold, outlining the heart perfectly. This disc picks up any sound and directs it toward their ears, which are placed asymmetrically and are of different shapes, so the owl is able to work out the exact location of a moving animal. They have the most sensitive hearing of all animals, and their necks can turn 270 degrees, which is necessary as their eyes can only look straight ahead. Their feathers are adapted for quiet flight; their foremost wing feathers have rows of tiny hooks that help deaden the sound of air. Their feathers are not waterproof however, which is why many die of hypothermia in a wet spring.

Having had a captive bred barn owl called Magik for many years, I recognise all of these details. However, there are things about owls the books don't tell you… that the down on a barn owls chest is the softest thing you can imagine, especially when the bird is nestling into your neck, and it smells wonderfully of old, of damp, of earth; that its eyes are a bottomless obsidian black that seem to look straight through you; that they move their heads from side to side when focusing, which gives them an almost comic appearance, and when threatened, snap their beaks to scare; that they have ticklish areas behind their ears, shutting their eyes, hunkering down and crooning; that they enjoy standing in the dogs' water bowl, screeching every time a dog dares come near; that contrary to popular belief, they are not wise; that they like to balance on your head and chew your hair and it's true their talons are the sharpest of sharp; and although almost weightless, they are full to the brim of owl things and belong to a liminal world. That they are the most beautiful of creatures.

~ *Time in a Garden* ~

The beginning of September and eleven years since we moved here. I'm sitting outside on the worn patio chair and it's that lovely end of summer warm which tastes of sea, suntan lotion and drying grass and which signals the children going back to school. There's a clatter of a tractor from a distant field and on-off low rumble from the quarry. A song thrush is tap-tapping a presumed snail against her anvil, a grey stone with a convenient bump mid-centre – I found a whirl of a coffee-and-cream empty shell by the side of the stone yesterday. Over to my right, the cherry tree still stands green with no hint yet of its autumn coat, and overlooks the hedge of holly and cherry plum, plus a few late flowers of the carmine pink rose Paul Ricault which weaves through them, leaning towards where the sun will set in a few hours' time. On the wall behind me and across the concrete floor, a run of black ants march in a one-ant width line, disappearing into a hole at the bottom of the wall. Opposite my viewpoint is the garden that was once a field and which is looking at its best in this waning sun. The light is softer, laying a gentling hand over the plants, the trees, the grass. Even the sounds are muted.

    The garden that was once a field is now full of ornamental grasses. Situated on the right of the drive before you reach the farmhouse and sitting just above the building, the field had originally been fenced and contained a small hut made out of local stone and corrugated iron and was used as an isolation unit for a sick cow. I pulled up the fence the first spring following our move before the grass had time to grow and planted a blush-white Mme. Alfred Carriere rose and twining honeysuckle to cover the hut. Five sinuous borders evolved over the next two years, which involved a lot of digging. The field grasses were replaced by ornamental ones – a prairie garden, so called.

Coming late into growth, grasses are at their best in this early autumn light. *Stipa Gigantea* throws up arching oat-like flower heads into the air. They can reach six feet tall and shimmer and dance with the smallest breath of wind. When you plant a statuesque grass, like Stipa, you want to plant it where it catches the light best from where you're most likely to see it, so from where I'm sitting, the sun is behind the plant, which catches and aflames the tiny seed heads and turns them to drops of gold. At its feet, a group of its smaller relations *Stipa tenuissima* or angel hair grass, tumbles and flows and turns in a river of buff-blond weaving through the garden, seeding wherever it likes. *Sedum* 'Autumn Joy' or stonecrop, a type of succulent, rests against the standing stone, its domed, pale green, fleshy flower heads, a collection of tiny pin-stars, just turning a pale raspberry pink. This plant is a bee and butterfly magnet, swarming with honey bees, bumble bees, peacocks and tortoiseshell. Alongside, the striking, steel blue stems of *Elymus magellanicus* or blue wheat grass spread around the stone and drift through the dry part of the garden. The soil here is only a hand's depth deep, furrowing along the ridges of shale and stone, so this grass is one of the only plants that could survive in this harsh site. I wasn't sure if it would survive, but it has thrived and is now spreading almost uncontrollably by means of long runners. There are very few plants that have such an unusual silver-blue colour. Further up the slope, on more fertile ground, the moor grass, *Molinia* 'Transparent' has rocketed into growth, bright green mounds of grass-like leaves supporting tall, feathery spikelets of brown, rice-grain seed heads, see-through and lace-fine. They tremble and bend, arcing to touch the ground when the dew lies upon them, each seed head glittering and gleaming with the sun.

Wind is a prairie garden's friend and wind abounds here.

Over to the right of the farmhouse and behind the old railway carriage, I've made two rectangular beds with railway sleepers, lined with the daggings from the sheep shearing, which help keep moisture in the soil and are full of nutrients such as nitrogen, magnesium and potassium. One of the beds is a herb garden, originally planted with the herbs from a song – parsley, sage, rosemary and thyme – interspersed with marjoram, chives, garlic chives and lemon balm. Mint has to be contained elsewhere. Over the last few years, everything has come together in a culinary chaos, which is fine as I don't cook as much as I used to. Lemon balm is my favourite herb for making tea, as it's good for reducing anxiety and for aiding sleep. It has a subtle, perfumed lemon taste and when it is in flower, the bees flock to it as well.

The other bed is planted with gooseberries, white, red and black currants, and autumn raspberries, mixed together like a summer pudding as I've been lax with the pruning. I used to make a few pots of redcurrant jelly and leave the rest to the blackbirds that nest nearby, and made pie or jam with the blackcurrants and gooseberries. The larder is still full of jam and jellies.

Opposite the back door to the farmhouse and in the triangular shaped border next to where I'm sitting, a fiery Virginia creeper or *Parthenocissus quinquefolia* clings to the wall behind with tiny padded feet. It spreads upwards and sideways, creating a wonderful backdrop of orange, gold and red in autumn, and provides a support to an unnamed yellow and pink flowered honeysuckle. Flowers of a scented, deep red climbing rose droop downwards over where I'm sitting – looking upwards is the best position to appreciate it. A bronze carex and *stipa arundinacea*, with misty seedheads of gold and umber glow and grow alongside almost black poppies, with pepper-pot seed heads of pale green, and a tall bronze fennel, whose feathery plumes invite you to touch them. They feel soft and moist and smell and taste strongly of aniseed and I use them instead of dill when cooking. The smell clings to your fingers for a long while. The strap-like leaves and curved stems of a golden flowered day lily contrast with the cerise, watermelon and copper butterfly flowers of rosa Mutabilis. Behind me, in large terracotta pots against the south facing wall, a tall whispering bamboo offers some shade, whilst the roses Grace and Gertrude Jekyll offer up a musk and old rose perfume and colours of apricot and fuchsia. This border was the first one I dug and planted, the digging more of an assault with a crowbar. I knew this would be the spot we would sit out on to eat, to drink, as it was the only level space near the farmhouse.

I don't know exactly why and when I started to love gardens, I just know I always have. Visiting gardens, plant nurseries or garden centres are happy places for me. I've made a garden in every house I've lived in, even if it had to be contained in a few pots. My parents and grandparents all gardened, not just for love, but also for food – growing your own back then was, for them, a necessity not always a pleasure. Homegrown potatoes, best cooked immediately and served with butter and a sprig of mint, also home grown; runner beans, my mum's favourite, eaten with lots of black pepper and bread and butter; broad beans, which I hated and still do; peas, which never made it as far as the kitchen. Rhubarb, blackcurrants and gooseberries, eaten in pies or crumbles, were staples. As well as the vegetables and fruit, there was always a sprig of flowers in an old jam jar, or a posy of in season flowers for the house – velvety-red and gold-bronze wallflowers whose rich colours made me want to stroke them and which smelt of warmth and honey; sweet William, spicy clove smelling rosettes in every shade of pink, maroon and white; lilac, pink and purple sweet peas, the scent of just one flower filling the room, and dahlias, which were not my favourite but always seemed to be grown in lines in the vegetable garden.

My first memory of the magic of growing plants from seeds was when aged seven, my sister and I were told we could each pick a packet of seeds to plant in the corner of the border in front of the house. After much deliberation, I chose *convolvulus tricolour* or dwarf morning glory, with trumpet shaped flowers in coloured rings of bright blue then white, with an egg-yellow throat, whilst my sister chose *Godetia* in frills of pinks and whites. I still remember the excitement of the first flowers opening as they corkscrewed their way through a nearby shrub.

Wrapping the house in greenery, in flowers, in abundance, being able to provide food for the insects, the birds, for us, a garden became another space to make my own, adding an extra layer to my sense of place. I didn't want to live being surrounded by another person's dreams, after all, most gardeners are dreamers. And nature, whatever that entails, becomes closer, more accessible when you have a garden. Caring for one makes you more aware of the seasons; which way the wind blows and what affect this has on the landscape; where the sun rises and falls; which parts of the garden flood in winter, or become baked-dry in summer. Which walls were welcoming to roses, clematis, and fruit, and which were wind-tunnels where every leaf would crisp and burn. You're more aware of the birds, how they fly and how they sing; which insects are safe to be with and which to leave alone; what flowers were the bees' favourites; how fertile the soil is judging by the number of worms working within it. It gives you a sense of achievement, creating something beautiful that fits and merges into the landscape as if it had always been there, even though there's little time to enjoy it as you're busy weeding, criticising, planning the next.

Maybe it was a control thing as well, which was ridiculous as you can't control a garden, you can only try to exert some form of order on the chaos. I could and did spend hours gardening – planning; drawing; designing; searching; reading, as well as time spent outside – digging; weeding; sowing; planting; taking cuttings; pruning; composting. I loved it all.

That changed when Dave died. Looking after a garden takes up so much time and time was one thing I didn't have when he became ill, so my borders started collapsing, initially in a gentle way. Grass grew in the borders, the creeping buttercups did what they did best, nettles weaved through rose and shrub and at first they just added to the misty greenness of everything when seen from a distance. The only time I saw things up close was during my weekly cut of the grass with the sit-on mower I'd bought when it became obvious I wasn't going to have the time to use the push mower, and then I drove quickly enough to ignore the signs of the weed takeover. Why did a few weeds matter anyway? But after a year, it was almost too late to halt the onslaught – it was if the eight years of my trying to mould the space had never happened. Football sized head of lime-green angelica towered alongside the burrs of burdock, whose huge, heart shaped leaves hid seedlings of bittercress – which spat out ripe seeds a metre away – plus herb bennet, oxalis and herb Robert. Brambles snuck in from the corners of the woodland and began to march gardenwards; sycamore and ash saplings grew feet overnight; couch grass stretched for the sun and threaded and twisted and forced its way through everything and the thuggish relation of my first grown convolvulus, the hedge bindweed, twirled anti-clockwise around anything it could, its moon flowers and heart shaped leaves belying its true nature as it strangled any smaller plant it came into contact with.

The unravelling of my beautiful garden reflected the unravelling of our life.

It took almost as long to restore some sense of the garden as it did to create it.

Time has a different flow in a garden. It shifts and bends, condenses, stretches out in front of you. Often, you think you have more time than you have. In the crucible of a garden, time lies all about you, not just in the day-to-day clock-time, but also in the deep time of roots reaching downwards into soil created over hundreds of years; the chronological time of those plants grown here for centuries, like the forget-me-not and the dog rose; the new time of the man-made F1 hybrid seed varieties, which cannot reproduce true to type; the historical time, where flowers have been used as emblems or symbols, like the yellow flag iris, which inspired the fleur-de-lys of knights and kings and was used on 14th century coins; plus geographical or world time, represented in the abundance of plants brought from overseas, like the maroon and purple matucana sweet pea, brought here in 1699.

To make a garden, you have to want to. It's hard work. You need a little knowledge of plants and soil and lawns, but that's easily done. A good garden centre or watching *Gardeners World* helps.

To make a good garden, you need to have passion, imagination, patience, love for what you're trying to create. And you need time. Time to do all the digging, the weeding, the pruning. Plus time to plan. What else is there to do on a dark winters evening apart from poring over seed catalogues and reading books and devising plant combinations? To make a good garden you have to involve all of the senses – vision, sound, touch, taste, smell – plus the feelings these evoke. Movement, light and shade, also play a part. Working with what you've got – the right plant for the right place – is vital. Otherwise you'll spend all of your time watering, moving, regretting. A good garden fits into the landscape as if it's grown there by itself, the plants seeding themselves in the perfect spot with no help from humans, something which is very difficult to achieve. A garden should have a personality of its own and it should make us feel something. Where does it take us? What story does it tell? How can we create a bit of magic in our own gardens?

There wasn't a garden when we moved here. Well, there was a space within the L shape created by the farmhouse and the cottage, with a small patch of grass, most of which had been covered by rubble and building flotsam due to the renovation of the cottage. The area was so dry and barren that a black redstart nested in one of the barns at the side the first year we were here, obviously mistaking the place for a cliff or a boulder field. Due to their booming population following the second world war, these birds became known as the 'bomb-site bird'. The birds are a similar size to a robin, but the male has soot-grey smudged feathers, a black face and a rust-red tail. The female is quieter.

How lovely to have one so close. They never came back once we started the renovation.

This 'garden' contained one fuchsia bush, one pittosporum, a lopsided conifer, plus a tall shrub that I couldn't identify but turned out to be a *Crinodendron Hookerianum* or Chilean lantern tree, which had large, strawberry pink dangling flowers in spring and looked like they were made out of plastic and were strangely beautiful. The setting was perfect however, facing south with a backdrop of small trees, and I could envisage creating a lovely garden there.

Which I did over time. It became the main rose garden, more formal than the rest, due to the square and symmetrical nature of the space. The main problem was the land sloped in one corner, so after the cottage renovation was finished I spent days wheelbarrowing in bought topsoil to even out the area and fill in the gaps left by the building works. And instead of the redstart, bullfinches came to take their place, dividing their time between here and Quarry field, both having backdrops of trees. Such beautiful birds, slightly larger than a well-fed robin, the males with a breast the colour of apricot-pink, a slate-grey back, and a cap and tail of black, the female being a more subtle version. I often spot one when they're flying away from me as their wings flash black and white, and occasionally hear their forlorn song through the undergrowth. Perhaps forlorn as thousands used to be killed annually because the birds like to eat the buds on fruit trees and also, like the goldfinch, they used to be captured and kept as cage birds.

It takes a lot of plants to fill a garden and plants cost money, so I sowed as many seeds as I could, even though it would be years for most of them to reach their full potential. I divided the plants I'd brought with me from Sussex, took cuttings from friends and neighbours, bought plants from village shows, plus some I found for sale at the side of the road. Things I'd always done to create a garden. Obviously, I went to plant nurseries and garden centres, as some of the plants I needed to use to create my vision couldn't be found in other people's gardens, but plants from others mean more somehow. By using cuttings from others, by asking for plants as gifts, you're then always reminded of the people that gave them to you, so they become part of your garden as well, as living memories.

Some of those are here, in this first tiny border I created the spring after we moved, next to where I'm sitting now. The Virginia creeper was a cutting from the last house we lived in and I'd taken that from a plant growing on my mum's garden wall. Her plant covered acres and was the result of a cutting she herself had taken from my gran's house in the 1960s which was situated in a blink-and-you'll-miss-it village in South Wales. Gran has been dead for 35 years but lives on in this clinging vine. The bronze carex and *Stipa arundinacea* I grew from seed and brought with me; the honeysuckle was a cutting from a friend's garden; the bronze fennel was sown from seeds collected in my old garden, as well as the almost black poppies. The day lily and Lady's mantle came from my mum's garden.

Dave had asked for a red rose, so Ena Harkness in her upside down, crimson glory is in honour of him; and the Gertrude Jekyll, Grace and Mutablis roses, I'd dug up and brought with me. The bamboo was a division of a huge clump of bamboo that encircled the Mother Superior's own garden within the original boundary of an old hospital where I used to work, which was eventually sold for housing. I'd loved working there and the bamboo reminds me of almost forgotten-but-not-quite mix of fellow staff and patients, many long gone. The purple-blue aquilegia, or Granny Bonnet, was a pale, spindly plant I'd found struggling for light in the old Cwm, crowded by grass and the overhang of trees and near to the old, ruined house, so I'd dug it up and planted it somewhere with more light. Had one of the old owners planted it there, in the protection on the walls around the house, I often wondered? If so, they would be happy to see it now. It has thrived, and has populated every part of the garden with flowers of pink, white and ink blue. It has found its place.

~ *Hedgehogs, Harvests and Moles* ~
(Cromlech field and Parc Penrallt)

> *...the whole sensation of rural Wales can be
> concentrated into one small patch of ground, a foot or
> two square, if that ground is Welsh enough...*
>
> (Jan Morris)

Autumn came late to Penbanc. Mid-October and many of the trees were still in leaf, apart from the sycamore, which always die early and badly, with curling fingers of leaves scorched at the edges, and the crack willow – many of its olive-like leaves falling before they had time to colour.

Today is the most glorious of days. The sun still feels warm against my face, but there is a tang of autumn in the air, of over-ripe apples, woodsmoke, blackberry jam. A brushstroke of white streaks against the bluest of skies; the hills as clear as cut-outs, the air crisp as a Granny Smith apple. The fact it might be the last of the blue skies before winter arrives makes it more special, more memorable even. I whistle the dog and walk past the stables that used to house the chicken and Guinea fowl before we moved them nearer to the house, hoping the fox might pay fewer visits. The neglected vegetable garden opposite is a reminder of my unusual inactivity over the summer, when I had little energy to do anything rather than get through each day. A few unpicked runner beans still cling to the wigwam Dave made from cut hazel branches years before and the remains of the plants are now brown and wrinkled. I know I should save the seeds to sow next year as I always used to, but don't have the enthusiasm to do so. Will I want to grow them in the new house? I can't think past the question. Maybe they won't want to grow somewhere new to them, perhaps they're hefted to here – their descendants have grown in this place for at least seven years. The undug onions have come into flower, tall, firm glaucous stems topped with globes of tiny white stars forcing their way skywards, and the rhubarb stems that I didn't harvest as there wasn't anyone to make rhubarb crumble for, have collapsed into a brown-pink mush surrounded by a circlet of collapsing leaves. The self-sown buddleia which fed the tortoiseshell and peacock butterflies in the summer and which, like its relations, is trying to take over the footprint of any available space, is the only thing that still looks healthy.

Under my feet the green lane between the fields is cracked and pitted, with deep grooves either side created from my habitual use of the quadbike which I use to give the sheepdogs a good run – there are no sheep for them to round up now. No matter how often I try to drive the bike on the edges of the ruts to squash the mud down, the path always reverts to the one it wants. Once a path has found its course, it stubbornly tends to stay that way.

There's a water trough in the gap along the knitted hedge of blackthorn and hazel. Each time I walk past it, I am reminded of the dead hedgehog I found last year, drowned in the deepness of the water, the straight, metal sides too steep for it to gain a purchase. I cried then and almost do now, feeling guilty that I hadn't come across the poor creature before and worried that there weren't enough water bowls around the farm for the hogs, even though deep down I knew there were plenty. Two autumns previously, one of the dogs brought a young hedgehog into the house and then proceeded to bring in two more. He hadn't hurt them – maybe he thought they were some kind of toy to play with. The hoglets were little coffee and cream spiked balls, and I picked one up carefully, resting it on its back, the spikes more like bristles when I touched them. It uncurled slowly, glass bauble eyes of brown-black and a tiny snout emerging from a soft beige belly. It was about half the size of an adult hedgehog, and I knew, having volunteered for a short time in wildlife rescue, there was no way it and its siblings would survive. The fact they were out in daylight, and on closer inspection, were more of an egg shape than an apple, meant they were dehydrated. It had been a dry summer.

Luckily, there was a hedgehog rescue centre nearby in Cenarth, so I took them there, where they stayed for a few weeks to gain weight, ready for the winter. A hedgehog has to weigh at least 600 grammes before hibernation so once they were eating sufficiently, I took them back to the farm, so they could sleep safely in an old rabbit hutch until I could release them in the following spring. Since then, I've always left shallow bowls full of water around the farm, just in case.

A huge holly bush with armfuls of reddening berries, as well as a head high hedge of gorse with a few mustard flowers clinging on between the prickles, funnel me into Cromlech field. The strange thing about Cromlech field, is that there is no cromlech within it. A cromlech can be a single standing stone or several of them, often with a flatter stone on top, such as the Pentre Ifan burial chamber, a few miles up the road. There are two such stones in the western hedgeline in Rhiannon's field, plus one near to the house that was presumably used as a gatepost as it has a hole through the top of it, something that's common in the local farms. Maybe they were originally in the middle of the field, where the hedge has been removed – on the old maps, the field is divided into two, Cromlech Isa and Cromlech Ucha. There is an unscheduled monument indicated on the north side of field in Shed field on the same map, but nothing sits in that place today.

Cromlechs are often sites of burials, and as I'm walking, I wonder why this field was chosen and what was it about this particular place that was special. There are no indications of what might have been here, not to me, anyway; no present monoliths to align with, no special hills or mounds. Although what was here those centuries ago would have been very different to today, and who knows exactly where the original site of the stones were situated. And what memories lie beneath my feet as I'm walking? Are there any bones or bodies? Other than the animal ones that occasionally appear as if by magic or dug up by foxes.

I follow the still distinct sheep track around the length of the field. Walking always grounds me, makes me feel connected to the life underneath, and there's a sudden awareness of that now, making me stop walking for a moment. My feet are resting on top of the skin of the earth, the pedosphere, with soil full to the brim with grass, clover, dandelion, daisy, buttercup, speedwell, dock, thistle and other seeds that are biding their time before they germinate. Plus worms, beetles and tardigrades, and fungi, ants and mites, and all those invisible threads that bind and creep and hold everything together. And further into the deep and the dark below, lie the hardness of mudstone, sandstone and shale of which this land is made. And all of this part of the place I love so much.

The dog barks, urging me forwards. A small patch of ragwort persists at the edge of one corner of the field, with daisy-like flowers which sparkle with the colour of sunshine. Dried ragwort is poisonous to horses but as none of the animals seem to eat it fresh it must be unpalatable. The plant is a magnet for insects and butterflies throughout the summer and is the foodstuff for the black and gold tiger striped cinnabar moth, whose bright colours act as a warning to things that want to eat them – the caterpillars absorb and store poison from the plant. The adult moth is unmistakable, with fan like wings of silken grey-black and ladybird red and can often be seen flying during the day. It's named after the red mineral cinnabar, an ore of the metal mercury. There is a Ragwort Control Act, which allows the authorities to order the owner of a field full of ragwort to destroy the plants, due to their toxic nature. I leave the small areas alone as they aren't going to be cut for hay, and more importantly, insects love them. Locally, ragwort, like badgers and hunting, is a sensitive subject.

Another maligned plant is the spear thistle, which thrusts from the ground like a botanical rocket. The flowering stalk can grow up to 1.5 metres, rising from a dinnerplate size rosette of aptly named spear shaped leaves, each lobe ending in a spike. Its flowers are rosy-purple, fluffy tops puffing from balloons of spines. Now, most heads are the husks of flown seeds, similar to those of the dandelion, and the plants reproduce by seed only, unlike its cousin the creeping thistle, which spreads by sending out shoots to colonise the field and which can be difficult to keep in check.

I'd walked half a lap before I noticed that there was something different about the feel of the field. Something was missing – and then I realised the last of the swallows had gone. Normally circling and cutting the sky above me, chasing insects stirred up by my feet and the dog, twittering and singing, today there was nothing. It's strange, but when you hear the same sound over and over again, you become accustomed to it, you only hear it on a sub-liminal level. Just like the calls of the swallows. It takes a while to realise that the sound has vanished. Over the last month, the swallows and the martins had been leaving in dribs and drabs, rather than gathering in a large flock on the overhead wires. I always feel a twinge of sadness when the last ones leave, and this year was no exception. Even though there were fewer of them than last year, they were such a presence on the farm, with their weaves and dives, their whistles and warbles. I was going to miss their company. The farms and barns felt empty and silent when they departed. On this last swallow day, as I call it, I always stop and take a moment to remember what had passed during the last year and wonder what will have happened by the time they arrive the following year. The only thing I did know was that I wouldn't be here to see them.

The day felt strangely quiet, and it wasn't just the lack of swallows. It was the sort of day when any sound seems amplified and echoed, with no breeze stirring the trees either, an unusual occurrence. It was almost as if the fields were holding their breath, as if waiting for something. The starlings had yet to arrive in any numbers and only the odd straggle of redwing and fieldfare had passed over, but they were too far away for me to tell the difference or to hear their rattling calls. For a few days only, without the presence of these migrants, the farm and woodland birds have the place all to themselves. How amazing are these migratory birds. They come, they go, and we have no real idea of the perilous journeys they undergo twice a year. How incredible that they return yearly to the same area, let alone the same nest site. And this country is home to the swallows, the swifts, the house martins, the chiffchaffs, the flycatchers – they raise their families here. Until recently, I hadn't considered the concept, the magnitude of these birds' own inherent sense of place. That their sense of place, this place, was the same as my own.

By chance, a red admiral butterfly rises from the ground in front of me and the dog runs to chase it. It's been feeding on the fallen apples littering this corner of the field. Such a vivid creature and easily recognisable; a sudden flash of black, white and red. When you look closely however, its black body is a sumptuous dark chocolate brown and there is a tiny forget-me-not blue dot on the bottom of the hind wings. The red is more of an orange and the French name for the butterfly is *Le Vulcain*, or The Vulcan, the god of fire, a name which sums it up perfectly. We think about birds migrating, but maybe not enough about the butterflies, of which the red admiral is one. They fly from Europe and North Africa during early summer until September, so by now there is a mixture of migrant and local butterflies. They can live up to ten months but rarely do so because of our cold winters. I watch it until it lands on another apple, snapping its wings shut so all you can see is a marbling of fawn, cream and brown, a mirror to the fallen leaves surrounding it.

This part of the field runs to the north and lies wetter than the rest. In spring, the new grass is sprinkled with sprays of the palest of pink and mauve and white cuckoo flowers, so called because they both arrive at the same time. The plant is also called lady's smock, or maids-a-milking, which is what I knew it as when I was growing up. It's one of the food plants for the orange tip butterfly, whose Belisha beacon wings announce spring. Trembling field buttercups and white clover follow on, a few of the clovers still in flower now, a finger touch of pink smudging the inflorescences of creamy white. The plant is food for the common blue butterfly, and was a good one for our sheep, as it has a high protein content and is very digestible. As a member of the bean family, clover is able to fix nitrogen in the soil, which is another advantage of growing it. Before intensive agriculture, bees foraging on clover plants produced three quarters of all British honey. But there are no bees flying or foraging today. It must be too cold for them now.

Feathers drift and catch amongst the stems of grass, pale grey and silver, and a few steps further lies a blizzard of white curls, which are probably the remains of a pigeon following a sparrowhawk kill – the feathers are intact, not torn or bloodied, which normally indicates a fox.

Following winter storms a few years ago, three racing pigeons appeared in the yard, recognisable by the ring on their legs. One stayed close for a few days, mingling with the home birds before disappearing, but I managed to catch the other two, placing them in an unused stable. They were easy to catch so must have been shocked or hungry. You are supposed to notify the society if you find a racing pigeon and give them the number on the bird's foot tag so the owner can be informed. These pigeons were friendly birds, obviously used to being handled, and one stayed on the farm for a month or so. I worried how it would survive, being a single bird flying without the safety of a flock and not used to searching for its own food. I was sad to see it go, especially as someone told me that their owners sometimes culled birds that turn up late as they don't want that trait in the bloodline, but I have no idea if that is true. Apparently, over fifty percent of birds fail to return to their loft, which is a staggering number of lost birds. Homing pigeons have been used to carry messages for centuries – Julius Caesar is said to have used them in his campaigns and they were used during the second world war – and racing for sport began in the 1820s. Pigeons were nicknamed the poor man's racehorse as it was then seen as a working-class activity. It is thought pigeons navigate to their home by using the earth's magnetic field, by recognising landmarks, olfactory clues, and the position of the sun. How vital is a sense of place to these birds.

We walk along the far end of the field, the dog circling and crouching low, rounding up imaginary sheep. The hedge here hasn't been cut in years, so it's a treeline, not a hedgeline. An old elder bends and bows low, clusters of black-purple berries drooping from its branches, a feast for the yet-to-arrive migrant birds. Although they look like they can be eaten straight off the tree, the berries have to be cooked before humans eat them as they contain small amounts of toxins, but I can never resist eating just one. Just because. However, they look more enticing raw than they taste – tart, sour, musky. Next to the elder, the roots of a looming holly have been exposed by generations of sheep that sheltered under it when the wind blew in from the north. They haven't been gone long enough yet for the bare, trampled soil underneath the tree to reseed. Dried pellets of black-brown pepper the ground, looking like oversized rabbit droppings.

We cross into the next field, Parc Penrallt – which means the head of the upper wood – through an old gateway whose sides have been created from stones picked from the fields, many with threads of white and rust crystal running through their veins, and which is collapsing in places. A larger crystal balances on top of the stones, which helps to protect the wall from evil spirits. This field has a different feel to Cromlech; darker, smaller, more secret, more hidden. The sheep never seemed to stay in here too long for some reason, preferring the upper pasture. Hawthorn and hazel lead the way toward the wood and at the entrance, a pale-breasted buzzard rises from the leaning fence post and flies low, wood gliding, its fingertips outstretched, feeling through the air. Touches of sunlight turn the edges of its wings to white gold as it lazily spirals and loops. A crow caws and follows, mobbing the bigger bird. They twist and roll and rise and fall again, the buzzard gaining height, but the crow's heart isn't really in the chase. It stutters and falls earthbound whilst the buzzard soars skywards with a flick of its wings, mewing twice as it circles higher and higher, until I lose sight of it. If he had had one, the buzzard would have been Dave's favourite bird. Years of not seeing any of them in Sussex due to illegal killing, pesticides affecting their fertility, and the drop in rabbit numbers – a food source – due to myxomatosis, meant they were still an unusual sight for him. I felt the same about the red kite.

Changes in human practices meant both of these birds were saved. These two birds demonstrate what can be achieved if there is enough will to prevent the decline of a species, the red kite in particular being near extinction in this country due to human behaviour. Seeing both birds gives me some hope that we can do the same for other birds and animals if the will is there.

The shivelight beckons me downwards and in a hollow in the hinterland between wood and field and near to where the crow sits hidden, an ash tree lies spreadeagled amongst the long grass. It fell three autumns ago, probably due to ash dieback which is affecting many ash trees on the farm and throughout the country. Most likely our own fault for importing ash plants from Europe. One tell-tale sign of this fungal disease is bareness in the trees' upper branches, obvious in high summer but not so obvious now when the leaves are starting to fall. It's been difficult to get anyone to move the huge trunk, so there it has stayed, growing greyer by the season, its smaller branches smothered by strands and knots of yellow grass and the choking wands of blackberry. Today, the trunk is surrounded by scatterings of milk-white mushrooms. I bend and pick one up. The rounded top feels cool and smooth, and it looks and smells like a field mushroom – a smell of the earth mixed with hazelnuts – but I can't be sure, so I leave the rest where they are.

The field is a larder of potential food. Golf ball crab apples, the colour of a Pembrokeshire sunset; sage-green hazel nuts hiding within a ruff of darker green; purple-black berries of blackberry and elder; pillar box of hawthorn, scarlet of rose and orange of rowan; spine-protected sloes, waiting for the frost to make sloe gin; plus the mushrooms. Even the chickweed that's scrambling up the bank can be eaten, leaves and stems reminiscent of a butterhead lettuce. In spring, primrose and violets nestle in the shelter of the foot of the hedges and years before I crystallised their flowers to put on top of a cake at Easter.

As the dog and I walk up the slight incline towards the gateway, a mistle thrush chatters and a robin flies onto a low branch of hawthorn. It begins to sing, the sound echoing through the clear air, following me up the hill. There's a melancholic strain to a robin's song in autumn, a wistful, silvery melody, different to the confident full-throated golden warble of spring. It's a song of the year coming to an end.

A week later, the trees' autumn shades arrive overnight. Yellow of birch; copper of beech; gold of field maple; red of hawthorn; tangerine of rowan; yellow-green of oak. The wind swirled them around in a cornucopia of colours, blowing them far from the trees in a couple of days. They drifted through the windows, filled the gaps in the barn doors, became stuck on the bottom of my wellington boots as I kicked my way through piles of them like a child. For a week they covered everything as if it was their last autumn.

Out early one morning, when strands of invisible spiders' webs caught against my hair and the remains of the sea mist clung onto the bare hedgeline in the lower fields, I found a dead mole in the middle of Cromlech field. Seeing a mole here was strange, especially as there wasn't a molehill in sight. There was only this black speck in the middle of a green field. When I came close enough, there was no visible mark upon the charcoal-black body, the paddle hands, the pink hairless snout, so there was no obvious answer to how it died. No smell of death clung to it either. Moles are smaller than I imagined, a hands length at most, and I'd only seen part of one previously which had presumably been caught by a cat. I'd seen pictures of them though, men standing with row upon row of dead moles when catching them was a job, hanging them in lines on a farmer's fence as evidence of their work. Strychnine used to be the preferred killing method but now they use mole traps; they sell them in the farm store. Farmers want to kill them because they can damage young plants and supposedly contaminate silage with listeriosis, and people want to kill them because they make unsightly lumps on their tidy lawns. Perhaps they've forgotten that moles, these fascinating creatures of the underworld plus a beloved character in children's books, the moldywarp, used to be here before us.

Moles need 50 grammes of earthworms a day to survive. They immobilise the worm by biting their neck segment – their saliva contains a toxin that paralysis them – then store them in a chamber underground. Moles are incredibly strong and are able to shift 500 times their own bodyweight and dig 200 metres a day. As they spend most of their time underground which has much less oxygen than at the surface, they have double the amount of haemoglobin and more blood than any other mammal their size.

I was unaware of these facts as I looked upon this dead moldywarp lying right in the centre of the field and found it strange that most of these facts I'd found were on a pest control website. Perhaps it's a case of knowing and respecting your enemy.

I wasn't sure what to do with the body, which looked like it had been left out as some sort of sacrifice. Perhaps it had. Should I leave it? Bury it? Put it underneath the hedge in the semi-dark? I just knew it didn't feel right, seeing it out in the open air when it should be sleeping underground. After all, moles are the guardians of the inner earth. I touched its coat, stroking the softness this way and that, a fur that had no nap and felt like expensive velvet. Strange to call it velvet when moles were around long before velvet was created.

In the end, I left it where it was. It seemed as if it had been left in the centre of the field for some unknown reason. When I returned the next morning, there was nothing there and nothing to indicate it once had been.

~ *Conker* ~

23rd October

When I was sorting out clothes to stay and clothes to go, I found a conker in the corner of a pocket of an old coat, the carefully designed pocket that's meant to hold a phone. It had slipped through the liner, a knobbly tactile thing. Into the air, pulled from its hiding place, it was covered in fluff, bird seed and other detritus that lurk in the bottom of pockets and handbags. Deep brown, surface dull as matt paint, a third of the size it once was.

I remember the day I picked it up, on a grey day of autumn. I'd collected handfuls for my granddaughter, too young yet to know the delights of how a conker felt, straight out of its nest of soft white, gently stroking with one small finger, the heart of a potential great tree.

I showed her how to twist a ripe one, how the two apple-green halves fitted together like a carefully constructed jigsaw. The surprise of the shiny brown conkerness nestling deep; a smell of newly picked apple and grass.

When I was a child, I would take handfuls of conkers home, the shells a ready-made box for trinkets, or as cups for toys, lined up alongside the fairy cups of acorns. I didn't realise the white of their inside would turn yellow, then a sludge brown, that the glossiness of my favourite conker – always one with circles of different shades of walnut, sherry, mahogany – would turn dull and flat, as if life was fading from it.

There was a favourite tree my dad would take us to, with candelabras of Neapolitan ice cream colours standing tall among leaves shaped like fans in spring and dripping with green sputnik capsules in autumn. The ground underneath would be littered with those that had fallen, hidden under brown-tipped leaves, like an old smoker's hand. Some had shed their contents, whilst others, the best ones, were ready to be popped open with a squeeze, nuggets precious as gold, with a sheen like my gran's freshly polished oak table.

The tree is still there, fifty-plus years older. It's aged more gracefully than me. I'd hoped to walk there, take my granddaughter to collect more conkers and even try to grow a tree from one of them, but the landowner has placed a fence around the field, so now we can only look at it from a distance.

~ *Fossils, Feathers and Stones* ~

When you come into the kitchen on a winter's day, you can feel the heat from the old cream Rayburn, full-up with kindling collected from the woodland floor, and when your eyes adjust to the dimness inside, you'll see a tall, old pine upright chest against the wall, situated at right angles to the table that Dave made two years before he died from old scaffold planks. The chest had been left in the wood shed, presumably destined for burning, and originally must have had a door as the rusty remains of hinges bleed brown down the right-hand side. The wood is battered and worn, the shelves bleached and marked, there are nails nailed in the oddest of places and the planks at the back have split because of the heat of the house, but I love the oldness, the sense of it. What did it used to hold, and how many people have placed objects upon those uneven shelves? They're perfect for placing large books that don't fit on a standard bookcase, and for keeping mementos I collected whilst out walking.

    I can't remember a time when I didn't collect things – pebbles, shells, feathers, a twig placed in a jam jar just waiting for a leaf to unfurl. As a child, I would return home from our annual holiday with buckets and pockets of the smooth iridescence of mussel shells, tiny peach and cream scallops, long pipe-cleaner tubes with hinges, grey and chalk-white whorls and spirals of empty homes. After a walk on the bleak and yellow grassed hillside above Merthyr, I'd come back with handfuls of gold. Fools gold, my grandad told me, not real gold, and people had lost fortunes over it. I didn't care as it was so pretty, glinting as I turned it this way and that in the light. During a fossil-hunting phase, the bottom of my wardrobe became covered with would-be discoveries that I'd try to sneak into the house without anyone realising. All these treasures being visual and tactile reminders of things I loved, or of places I'd been.

It's only recently I've realised that the treasures that have survived years of house-moves are the ones that tie me to a certain place, geographically and emotionally. They're reminders and links to things I've left behind, and which, for a brief moment, take me back in time as soon as I look at them or pick them up. And when I leave here, they will all travel with me again.

Today on the old pine shelves are a few objects that mean the most, grouped together almost without thought. The first is a fossil. Originally, I thought it was a starfish, but research has informed me it's a sea urchin – an 'irregular echinoid' named *Holectypus*, and is between 65.5 and 200 million years old, which I find quite incredible, especially as I found it many years ago amongst pine trees on a mountain near Valencia in Spain. It's about three inches across and is the colour of putty, striated like a snake and resembles a starfish sunbathing over a rounded rock. In technical terms, it is bun-shaped with a flat bottom and an arched back, the hollow underneath is called the oral surface and has a small depression which was its anal opening. Even though the surface is gritty and coarse, its curve makes it quite tactile and it fits snugly in my palm. It brings with it the burn of the sun and the menthol-freshness of the pines, the path slippery underfoot with the dry dust of the mountain and dead needles, the call of cicadas piercing the blue, and the memory of the person who was with me that day and who I would marry, the person who made the table the fossil lies next to.

Scatterings of sea-glass – glass shards tumbled by the incessant action of the waves – surround the sea urchin. Their sharp edges have become smooth and their clear surface frosted. They gather dust easily, especially wood dust from the Rayburn, so I often return them to water for a clean. They are more alive when submerged; their colours more pronounced. Due to the increase in recycling, these 'mermaids tears' are becoming more difficult to find. It takes between seven to ten years for a glass shard to become a tear. Orange is the rarest colour and white and brown the commonest. My favourite are the blue and green shades – the dark-blue from the cobalt in medicine bottles made in the 1880s and 1950s; the green from Sprite, 7-up and bottles that once held spirits; and one called sea foam, which has a colour exactly like its name, and which are the remnants of old Coca-Cola bottles. I collected them all from the seaweed-full tide-line of Ceibwr Bay, which is two miles from here as the gulls fly, and one of the reasons we wanted to live here. Touching their cool smoothness anchors me back there, reminding me of the sounds and smells of the sea and the times we used to walk there.

Alongside the sea urchin is an acorn-sized, irregular shaped terracotta stone, so rough to touch it would mark your skin if you pressed hard enough. Its matt surface is pitted with tiny holes and if you hold it really close to your nose, you get a sense of heat, of burning. I picked it up from the slopes of Mount Etna in Sicily, an otherworld, barren, inhospitable, mesmerising, moonscape of a place. Below the active part of the volcano, the land gradually changes from brown, sienna and orange to a lush greenness. There's a rainbow explosion of growth due to the mineral-rich volcanic soil, which gives life to a cornucopia of grapes and olives, aubergines and pistachios, lettuce and lemons, peaches and tomatoes. The local honey smells and tastes of oranges soaked in sugar-syrup and sun, and we dribbled it over bread fresh out of the oven, mouths and fingers sticky with sweetness, and ate it with cool, thick, white yogurt served in shallow earthenware bowls, during one of our last holidays together.

I have two stones that take me back to the place where we lived for many years. I picked them from the beach at Normans Bay in East Sussex and they are flinty cream and beige and grey and have a hole right through them. Known as hag stones, adder stones or snakes eggs, the holes are caused by the attrition of water, an adder, or from the tongues and hardened saliva of a large number of serpents massing together, depending on your beliefs. In Wales they are called *Glain Neidr* and were highly prized by the druids. They were considered to be magical because of their link with water, offering protection, healing and help with fertility problems and it was believed you could see the fairy world if you looked through the hole. If you thread a red cord through the hole and wear one around your neck during Samhain, it will work as a charm, or if you tie it to your bed, it will prevent you from having nightmares, according to legend.

One I use as a pen holder, as the hole is a perfect pencil-thickness, and the other holds a collection of feathers – the forget-me-not blue from a jay; the black and white spots of a woodpecker; the chocolate brown and cream of a buzzard's wing; a precious soft-white, amber and grey memento from my own barn owl, Magik: an iridescent mallard-green curl from my Pekin cockerel, picked up the day before the fox took him.

~ *Leaving* ~

The weekend before I left, storm Arwen made an appearance, and what an appearance it was. Hail, large and as hard as gobstoppers, littered the ground, stinging and sore where they made contact with skin. Squalling, buffeting rain battered the farm buildings all night, lifting the corners of the roof that weren't already weighed down with tractor tyres. The grate of metal on metal was never ending, one of those ear-wincing, teeth on edge sounds, a sound so regular that I found myself anticipating the next one.

The wind was a dreaded north easterly, I could tell by the way it hit my bedroom window, rattling the wooden frames and causing the blinds to sway, despite the two-foot-deep window ledge. In my bedroom at the back of the house, I can't tell when the wind blows from another direction – it blows over the side of the farmhouse if there's a southerly, and the stand of ash and sycamore trees between First field and Gwair absorbs the worst of a westerly.

It was wind from this direction that brought down Magog earlier in the year, so I went out the following morning with trepidation. The heavy wooden bench normally lying next to the kitchen door had been blown across the drive, whilst the wicker one was upside down in Gwair field. The gravel from the bottom part of the drive had been relocated to the front of the barn below and had made a perfect miniature beach, damming a small amount of water. Nature had already adapted to the change and the sparrows were drinking from this new pond whilst a squirrel hopped its way over this new barrier. Luckily, it wouldn't take long to push the gravel back where it belonged. Soggy fragments of dirty white pampas grass were scattered everywhere as I cracked my way up the lane, and silver-green moss dusted ash and sycamore branches littered the drive. Luckily, there were no fallen branches wider than the width of my arm. Although the wind strength had dropped slightly, checking the woods and the fields for damage wasn't a good idea. Not yet. Branches can fall anytime, especially from the trees affected by ash dieback – they fall without warning even in the calmest of days.

The hedges either side of the drive protected me from the worst of the wind, but when I reached the five gates, the wind swirled and danced, whipping the long grasses which smelt surprisingly like hay – the wind must have the same drying effect as the sun. The gates were singing, an aeolian sound which I fancifully took to mean they were saying goodbye. Overhead, fast moving, billowing clouds of murky grey, tumbled and twisted against a sea-green sky. A scattering of small brown birds flew in front of me, keeping low and close to the hedge and a lone mistle thrush stood still for a brief moment, head held high, body erect, its ink splattered chest puffed like a pugilist.

The field opposite lay an unusual spring-green compared to the usual dun and beige of the surrounding winter fields, the result of cattle slurry being spread during the last month. A flock of gulls, white, flint, charcoal, wheeled and turned and dived searching for food, their mournful, mewing calls cut short as the wind carried their voices ahead of them.

As I turned the first corner, the wind gentled slightly. At head height, a tiny, pink herb robert flower, a pale version of its summer self, sheltered under an edge-crusted dandelion leaf, the only plant of colour along the bareness and muted colours of the winter hedge and bank. Further down the lane, the squat Southdown sheep with grizzled, teddy bear faces were feeding on pale, green cabbages which had been scattered over the turf, and a small group of starlings startled over the hedge, chattering and clattering over my head. They were only a foot or so above me, and I stopped still amongst the whoosh of their wings as they headed towards the slurry field. For one joyous moment I felt part of them, could almost feel their hearts beating, felt part of something else that was greater than the sum of each individual bird. The memory stayed close for the rest of the day.

A fallen tree prevented me from going any further. It's predictably a willow. In the distance, half of the roof has blown off a neighbour's barn.

Three days before I left…
I woke early. The sky was beginning to lighten, streaks of red and pink against gold. It had rained again in the night, the wind still coming from the north. I didn't mind. It suited my mood. Standing outside the kitchen door, a tawny owl called from the wood and through the lightening, the ethereal figure of a barn owl effortlessly glided along the dark line of the hedgeline. I hadn't seen one for two years, and now there were two owls within yards of each other. I'd like to think it was some kind of omen, I just wasn't sure what sort of omen it was. It was something else that made me want to stay.

A blackbird called from the blackthorn. It was too dark to identify the tree as blackthorn, but after eleven years of passing it every day, I knew it was. The red morning sky had promised rain and it arrived around two, the same time as the future owner's sheep. They bucked and jumped like lambs, exploring their new home. Even though I'm not a farmer, the field looked better with sheep in them. Perhaps I've been living here alone for too long. The starlings liked the sheep too, it wasn't long before they arrived with a swoosh and a screech. Their flocks are smaller now, more fragmented than when they arrived. They save their patterns and murmuration for their roost at the marshes along the Teifi. The gloam of the rain made dusk appear early.

The day before I left…
More rain. It's why Wales is so green. The early morning sky swirled in charcoal and violet with orange flashes. A red kite cruised over first field,

rudder tail tilting. There's a large, white discarded crane bag in the middle of the field and for a moment, I thought it was a dead sheep. Perhaps the kite thought so too.

I took the quad bike out for the last time to see the fields. They were imprinted on my mind anyway, so there was no reason to look in every nook and cranny – it's what I've been doing since the farm was sold and there was nothing new to be seen. I've never liked the concept of 'making memories' for memories sake. However, there were a few specific things that needed doing today – I wanted to leave the farm early the next day, get the leaving done.

In Rhiannon's field, I placed my hand on the fallen cromlech to bid it goodbye, the quartz cool to touch, even in the early winter morning, the leaning apple tree nearby now nearly touching the ground. A flurry of redstarts and fieldfares were searching for the last of the berries from the holly tree and the rowan. I said goodbye to my favourite trees – it was still impossible to have just one. The sycamore standing alone in the hawthorn hedge, a perfection in symmetry; the silver birch that leant over the path that lead down to the old Cwm, the bend in its trunk the perfect height for hugging, its trunk whiter in places where I'd peeled away some of the bark; the sycamore you look down on further along the same path, that we'd nicknamed the magic faraway tree after the children's books; the twisted and gnarled oak in the new Cwm, where the veil between worlds is thinnest; the ash over the deck, where I'd lain underneath and watched the leaves make patterns against the sky, bringing me some form of peace in my grief filled world; Gog and the remains of Magog.

I went through my coat pockets in anticipation of the move; three coats in various stages of use. One had belonged to my dad and was far too big, which was useful in winter when I had to wear at least two jumpers. In the pocket that was supposed to hold a mobile phone, I kept my penknife and one of Dave's old sheepdog whistles. I'd kept it even though it had been pointless to try and instruct the dogs as they always ignored my poor attempts. They only took notice of him. But I kept it anyway. In my usual walking-the-dogs coat and amongst a mass of dog biscuits, orange baler twine wound in and out between an acorn; a shell, ridged-rough and the colour of travertine that I'd picked up from the strandline of Ceibwr Bay; an unidentifiable leaf, once green, now crumbling in beige, that I'd kept to try and identify; a scrap of paper with a scrawled few lines of poetry, now barely readable, and a flat black pebble found on the edge of the stream running through the cwm. I've always had the habit of picking things up and pocketing them, making a collection. These objects had made a collection by themselves, and they anchored me to this place in ways that no one else would understand.

In the afternoon, I stopped cleaning the kitchen sink to look at the last day of my world through the frame of the window. Four jays were squabbling over the peanuts in the feeder, scaring even the squirrel away. Two greater spotted woodpeckers were running up and down the cherry tree, trying to get a look in, and when I banged on the window to scare the jays away, a slate and peach nuthatch saw his opportunity, stabbing at the nuts with its kingfisher beak. Five iridescent starlings were arguing over the fat balls, whilst the magnificence of a cock pheasant, an escapee from the pheasant farm up the road, sat under the apple tree, waiting for leftovers. I hoped the new owners would continue to feed them.

I was going to miss them all.

Last day…
I'd had a door made to fit in the gap between kitchen and utility room. It was a thing of beauty; smooth, pale, spalted beech, with darker knots and folds, rough to the touch. I ran my hand over the warmth of the wood one last time, before pulling it to, gently. I'd thought about taking it with me, but decided it was part of the farm. Like a lot of things I'd decided to leave. Some things belong to places not people.

I'd wanted to have a last look around, but the buyers' removal men came early. Some things you need to do by yourself, in the silence of the place that holds you, so perhaps that was a good thing. My time had run out.

I'd been dreading locking the back door; it made everything seem final. It reminded me that when we moved in, there wasn't even a key to the door. But as others were here, there was no need to lock it. I could pretend I was taking my daily walk up the lane; the door was never locked then. And there was a sense of things unfinished, somehow. Like I was coming back. Or perhaps that was just wishful thinking.

~ *Footsteps* ~

I walked in the memory of your footsteps today.
It felt the same as when you went away.
Clouds hung heavy on the horizon, no
breeze stirred the leaves
on the sycamore trees.
The stream meandered its way home
pausing to reflect under weeping willow and
chattered with dipper and wagtail under the old stone bridge,
hart's tongue fern and moss laden.
The sun dripped pale yellow along its path to the sea and
a boot mark caught by the autumn rain
sparkled.

The gate was half open, expecting you to close it, and a
wayward stem of dog rose trembled, hoping to catch you in its embrace.
It waited all summer… then
slowly withered and died when it realised you weren't coming back.

~ *Moving Forwards – A Day in a Life* ~

*Someone said there were seven stages of grief
as if you had to pass each stage
before you go onto the next and
finish all sparkly and new.*

Grief isn't like that.

*Grief waits to catch you unawares,
appears when you're least expecting it,
when you're driving, shopping or waking.
It seeps into every aspect of your life,
taints the food you eat, the air you breath,
the books you read.*

*There are no stages of grief.
There is just grief.*

March 1st 6.30am.

There's a blackbird singing outside the window, a melodious but melancholy sound. Its fluting and warbling is the only thing to be heard in the early hours of this suburban landscape. It's the first of March, and is also the first day of spring, Pancake Day and St. David's day – his patron saint – all in one. Dave would have been 58 in 27 days' time.

The light is edging around the borders of the new blackout curtains. Two months here, and I'm still trying to adapt to this new place, this cooler, taller, noisier, slanted ceiling place. I've positioned the bed so I can look across the fields that span like an emerald fan behind the garden when I wake up. Sheep were grazing, the grass October-bare, when I'd looked around the house three months previously, reminders of the farm I was having to leave. There was even a familiar tumbledown barn in the corner of the field, its corrugated orange and brown roof peppered with holes. The sheep were fat, Lleyn-types, similar to the ones we used to keep, and I could almost imagine they were ours. At least it wouldn't be me getting up at midnight to help with lambing.

I find the first of each month more difficult than the rest of it. For as long as we'd been together, I'd been woken up with a 'pinch and a punch, the first of the month', always around six o'clock, as he would always wake up far too early, even at the weekends. A childish habit maybe, but it was his thing and it made him laugh. And me, occasionally.

I've missed about 30 pinch-punches, and sometimes, like this morning, I do it to myself, just because.

I get out of bed, pull open the curtains and stare across the fields, the emerald swathe now winter-brown. No sheep today, just a handful of crows and a buzzard digging for worms – it's a lean time of year for them. There'll be more food around when lambing starts. I notice three sticks glowing orange in the middle of the field, bright amongst the mounds of earth tumbled by moles. I presume they're signs that traps have been laid. I like living in the country, but I don't like a lot of man's involvement in it. There are many aspects of a farm life I won't miss.

The sky is a translucent pearl colour, ribboned with peach, and the sun is just rising – a silver runway across the sliver of sea I can see through the trees. The naked arms of the oak trees stretch skyward with no bend to the east – the wind blows differently here.

It's never dark at night here either, not Pembrokeshire dark. Across to the north, the sky tints Swansea-orange and the lights on the road halo light. I can just about make out the stars, but they're faded and seem more distant somehow, but the Plough still sits above my left shoulder when I come out of the back door so at least that's familiar.

I climb back into the warm cocoon of the bed and press the on-button on the Teasmade that Dave bought for me too many birthdays ago, the white plastic now marked like coffee mixed with cream. No matter how hard I scrub, I can't get the stains out. I try to ignore the warning feeling of butterfly wings in my stomach and concentrate on listening to the hiss and splutter of the water beginning to boil whilst breathing deeply and slowly. After two minutes, I lean over the other side of the bed and pour the tea into my cup, moving back to the warm side of the bed to drink it. Two and a half years on and I still can't sleep on his side.

A wave of what I now know is anxiety begins; a combination of nausea, a dry mouth combined with a compulsion to swallow a lot, and a feeling as if someone is sitting on my chest making it a struggle to breathe. The heart palpitations haven't started yet, much to my relief, so I try to concentrate on taking measured breaths, watching my stomach rise and fall with each one.

Even through necessity I've learnt a few techniques which are supposed to help with these sensations and prevent them from getting worse, I frequently find they don't. Anxiety made its appearance about six months into Dave's illness, although illness doesn't describe the horrors of a terminal diagnosis. The anticipatory grief I'd experienced before Dave's death is a common complaint amongst those who live with someone who has a limited time to live. It's a reflection of the knowledge that your loved one is going to die, and there's nothing that you or anyone else can do about it. For me, it was made worse by the fact that Dave, as in the Dave I'd known, the Dave I'd fallen in love with, was changing. He'd became a different person to the one I'd known for 30 years. The tumour that was inexorably invading his brain was changing the essence of him, and that made it increasingly hard for all of us. The tumour that was killing him killed him long before the actual event. He became more introspected and said hurtful things. Even though I knew it was the tumour talking, it was still hard to deal with. The increasing number of steroids he was taking made him swell up, which made it difficult for him to breath and to walk far. He even lost interest in his beloved dogs, which was something we never imagined would happen.

At first my own feelings of anxiety were an irritation, something I tried to ignore, as after all, it wasn't me that was going to die. This was until the constant adrenaline rush started to cause physical symptoms which became impossible to ignore, and I ended up in hospital with an irregular heartbeat and symptoms of a heart attack. I was told, bluntly, to look after myself otherwise I could become ill as well.

Broken Heart Syndrome, or Takotsubo cardiomyopathy, is an actual condition and occurs when a person experiences acute stress, due to bereavement, accidents, or natural disasters, and causes reversible heart muscle weakness. It apparently is most common in post-menopausal women over 55 years old, so I was ticking lots of those boxes that medical staff seem to like. I surrendered, and listened to the people that supposedly knew what they were talking about, and began taking the inevitable chemical solution, reasoning that I would be able to stop taking the drugs sometime in my future. I did, but didn't realise at the time how hard this was going to be.

When I eventually made time to see a grief counsellor, she told me that in her experience, anxiety was the missing stage of grief, and that for most of her clients following a bereavement, anxiety was the most common symptom, something not generally recognised by the medical profession. We became anxious because the world as we knew it, had ended, with not just the loss of a loved one, but the loss of a supposedly known future and all the hopes and dreams that contained. Our sense of safety and stability also becomes lost, as someone's death is a reminder of our own mortality.

I became used to feelings of an understandable, overwhelming sadness, a sadness that pervaded every minute of every day, days that were so long as I couldn't sleep, as well as the physical manifestations I've mentioned. There was also an underlying sense of dread, plus waves of grief that came out of nowhere and felt like an actual blow to my stomach – the so-called sledgehammer of grief – which made me collapse onto my knees and just crouch, forehead on the ground, gasping for air like a fish out of water until the wave passed. However, anxiety was a new and unwelcome symptom, and until the counsellor explained, I couldn't understand why I felt anxious all of the time – grief, yes, anxiety, no. The most helpful thing she did, was firstly, to tell me that these feelings were normal and to be expected, and secondly, that contrary to widespread belief, you don't 'get over' grief. There was no magic timeline when I'd feel better, I would just learn to live with it and grow around it. This made a lot of sense, albeit an unwelcome one.

It still feels strange to talk about Dave in the past tense. He was so full of life – six foot three with a personality to match – and was one of those people that made an impact wherever he went. You'd notice when he came into a room. And sometimes, I still feel it difficult to believe that he's not in this world, somewhere, as if it's all been a mistake. It's been a long two and a half years without him in it, but although there are some days when I don't feel I've moved on at all, there are a few when I sense a brightening around the edges.

Nature had a great deal to do with this 'brightening'. It's too dramatic to say it saved me, but it shifted the focus away from myself and onto other things. As my world shrank even further, I began to focus on the minute, to ground myself in them and the day-to-day differences I observed in nature. I began to take pleasure in the smallest of things – snowdrops pushing their way through the iron-hard soil; daffodils dancing; the blue of a jay's feather left under the apple tree; the first bright green leaf of a hawthorn unfolding; the wash of bluebells under the oak trees; the return of the swallows. Birds in particular were a source of comfort, especially as the countrywide lockdown meant I hardly saw anyone. When grief took over, birds were always there to distract, to enjoy, to look after. If nothing else, I had to get out of bed to feed the birds.

I missed them more than I thought I would when I moved here. Birds had been a constant in my life for years; a daily connection with nature; their song a joy, a blessing, a given. So one of the first things I bought was a bird feeder, a black, shepherd's crook contraption with a number of hooks and bowls. It took three days for the first birds to appear – two blue tits and a baker's dozen of sparrows. I like sparrows, like their chattering, brown noisiness. A group of sparrows is called a quarrel, which describes them perfectly. It seemed as if this was a call for other birds to join the group, as within days, many other varieties appeared: robin, great tit, chaffinch, long tail tit, thrush, dunnock, collared dove, jay, starling, nuthatch, greater spotted woodpecker, goldfinch, the rare, coral smudge of a bullfinch, as well as my beloved blackbird. One day, a red kite soared over, conker-brown and white, tail angling with the wind, although this bird was on the lookout for dead lambs, not peanuts. We used to see so many of these beautiful birds cruising the hedge line on the farm, and of course the one that nested in an old oak tree not far from the house for a few years. It stirred memories to see a red kite here.

At night, I occasionally hear the unmistakable call of a tawny owl and another replying, echoing from the stand of oak and ash trees at the end of the lane, and I'm hoping there might be a barn owl living in the tumbledown barn, although this is probably wishful thinking, as they are so scarce. I had to leave my captive owl, Magik, at the farm as I didn't want to stress her by moving her. It would be lovely to see a wild one here.

Birds as well as nature, seem to have been a lifeline to many during lockdown, including myself. When I was able to return to reading, I read a number of reasons why birds had become important. They are a visible and audible connection with a natural world that a lot of people have lost a connection with, and they fit into our lives as there is a routine to their behaviour – most wildlife run away from us, but if we feed the birds, they come towards us. Birds are able to take us away from ourselves as we watch them, and then they ground us and bring us home. The sound of birdsong is reputed to make us feel happier.

Of all the birds, blackbirds hold a special place. They are the first birds I hear in the morning and the last thing I hear at dusk. One sits in the overgrown pittosporum tree that peers into my bedroom window and even though I can't see the bird, there's no doubt it's there. They were one of my dad's favourite birds – he was an avid birdwatcher – and most of my childhood and adult memories of him revolve around birds and visiting various places to watch them. He died six months before Dave and at his funeral, we played "Blackbird" by The Beatles. At the end of the tune, there are a few bars of a real blackbird's song so every time I hear the bird, I'm reminded of my dad.

Losing Dave and Dad within six months of each other was hard. My grief for each became tangled up into one big mess of loss. Mum and I became widows at similar times, and I don't know if this made it easier or harder for us to cope with. It did mean that we had an understanding of what the other was going through – the endless paperwork; not knowing where the stopcock for the water was; how to alter the timing for the central heating; having to tick the 'Widow' box on forms.

I still find this difficult, and I think that's when it truly hit me, when it became real. I could still call myself Mrs, but I was no longer married; my husband was dead. My marriage, like Dave's life had ended. I could always tick the 'Single' box, as, after all, I was single, but technically I wasn't – I was a widow. And by ticking that box, it was just another affirmation that Dave wasn't coming back.

Moving on – that worn out cliché. But it has to be done, no matter how slowly. Routine, and focusing on tiny things is another way I've found helps. I like to make time to have one 'proper' cup of coffee in the day, one of those habits I'd started to help ground myself. I make it in the cafetière I'd bought for Dave one birthday, although my one shot Americano with lots of milk is very different to the multiple three shot espressos he'd loved. I always drink it in a thin china cup Dad had bought me years ago. It's painted with pictures of birds – nuthatch, jay, coal tit, lapwing, with a tiny blue tit on the rim and I'm terrified of breaking it, so I hide it in the back of the cupboard so no-one else can use it.

I sit and look out at the garden whilst I'm drinking it and always make sure I've biscuits or cake to eat with my coffee as well. Not that I need any excuse to eat them but taking the time to make an occasion of it, is another tool, another routine, to help move the day forwards.

Whilst I'm sitting, I make a mental note of what's flowering or coming into leaf. There's not a lot at this moment, apart from a large pot of daffodils that I dug up and brought with me. Dave had loved daffodils, and these ones had been growing outside our kitchen window and were also scattered along the lane and throughout our neighbours' gardens. They are unusual in that each year the flowers are different – sometimes double, sometimes twisted and curled and when the weather is cold, they often turn green. They're called Van Sion daffodils and were introduced over 400 years ago. I've always thought them a beautiful link to the past. I planted some on Dave's grave before I left.

I'm planning what I'd like to do with this new garden. The space is very different to the last. I've begun to think that garden planning is a little like writing. Everything has a backstory; different voices/plants are present at different times, and you want a variety of them; you need a mix of colours, scents, texture, even taste. You need space as well as content and you have to look at the garden from all angles as you need a rounded point of view.

I'm already missing our garden, blowsy and informal, with trees dripping with roses and clematis, and just a sprinkle of weeds in the borders. I miss the hours spent outside, planning and planting whilst Dave did the digging, and the usual poring over seed catalogues, deciding on what to grow – *Sungold* or *Gardeners delight*, *Marmande* or *Costoluto Fiorentino* tomatoes; *Jalapeño* or *Bhut Jolokia* chillis; *Jersey royals*, or *Pink fir apple* potatoes – and growing too many plants and trying to squeeze everything in somewhere. I'll try not to remember how everything changed when he became ill and I lost all of my energy and enthusiasm, how his vegetable garden became strangled with brambles and nettles, and the lawn returned to the hay meadow it once was. How the garden became a reflection of our lives.

That needs to change. I want and need to try and get back into gardening here, to immerse myself in seeds and digging, to feel the soil between my fingers, make compost, grow food. I'll spend a few months looking at the plants already here and see what the soil is like before deciding what to do. Be patient for a while. I know the pittosporum tree at the back of the garden is far too big for the space it's occupying as it should be a shrub, not a tree. It'll probably have to be cut down soon, but I'll leave it this year. For now, I'll enjoy the honey-scent that'll drift over the garden through an early summer evening. You hardly notice the flowers that give off such a strong perfume; tiny and chocolate-purple. They'll attract the bees and butterflies that I want to encourage in this otherwise sterile space, which has been designed for maximum effect with minimum effort, with its shrubs carefully pruned into lollipops and squares, and all potential flowers and berries sheared off for convenience.

I've brought with me a fig tree growing in a pot and it resembles a collection of sticks at the moment. I'll plant it somewhere sheltered and where the soil is dry. Figs fruit best when their roots are restricted so where wall meets soil is ideal. I'd bought two plants as a reminder of a holiday we had in the Gorges de Verdon in France five years ago. One we planted at the farm, which fruited the last two summers – Dave had left a gap between the slabs when he'd rebuilt the patio and it had taken off with abandon – and this one, still in a pot. Figs were one of the region's specialities and we ate them in various incarnations : with goats cheese and honey, or walnuts; fig tart, which they ate at breakfast and was far too sweet for me; fig jam, spread on homemade bread with salted butter; figs with ham; or simply by themselves, which was how I preferred them, picking one straight from the tree, in the post-siesta sun, then putting my thumbs through the fragile skin and pulling the twilight-mauve fruit apart, and just eating, the juice running down my chin and my fingers.

The ones I ate last summer didn't taste quite the same. Perhaps they need the Mediterranean sun to give their best. Or maybe, who you're with and where you are makes a difference to how you perceive things.

The three, gnarled apple trees at the side of the garden are the only things that haven't been pruned into submission, and on one of the trees, a tiny bracken is growing, it's foot firmly wedged in the vee of two branches. It reminds me of the bracken and ferns growing on the oak trees in our old woods. The apple trees are as wide as they are tall and are covered in silver-green lichen and moss, which spring back when you touch it. A female blackbird sits on one pulling off beakfuls, presumably to build a nest. At least the trees will attract the insects and bees when they're in flower, and more insects means more birds, and more bees means hopefully more tomatoes – about 80 percent of the tomatoes we eat are pollinated by bees.

Dave and I spent our honeymoon in Normandy, which is full of orchards, deserted beaches and dairy farms. One night, we stayed in an old farmhouse and had breakfast with the family the next morning. Nearly all of the food we ate was produced by them, including apples in various disguises – apple puree, to mix with the homemade yogurt; apple cake; apple jam on croissants; home grown bacon and eggs, all washed down with apple juice. The breakfast that day was one of the best I'd ever had. I remember we ate far too much, maybe because we'd drunk too much of the home-made cider the day before. However, I'd woken without a headache, maybe because it was produced only a tree's length away from where we drank it.

Food and memories of meals we'd had seem to hold a large place in my memories of us. We'd both loved different cuisines, and I'd enjoyed cooking, inviting people over, experimenting. I hardly cook anything now. I can't get my head around cooking just for me, I don't enjoy it, although I still buy too much food – just in case – and end up freezing everything. I've shelves of cookery books, gathering dust. I'm hoping I'll rediscover my cooking self, alongside my gardening one.

Like cooking, reading was something that grief made impossible. I couldn't concentrate on anything, not even the gardening magazines my sister would buy me. It was a strange, almost unbelievable feeling. I have no memories of not reading. Books, in all their forms, had been such an integral part of my life. I remember in a school report, my English teacher had said I didn't read books, I devoured them, and this continued to be the case. In the days before kindle, I'd go on holiday with a suitcase full of books, at least one for every day away, instead of clothes. Now I couldn't read a page, had no interest in even trying. A close friend who I'd been in a book club with would come around and leave a book before she left. 'I've just read this,' she'd say, 'you might like it.' Or 'I've bought two by mistake, see what you think…'

I appreciated the kindness of the thought behind it so much. She was aware of how much reading had meant to me, but I found it hard to think about anything. However, it was one of the books she suggested, that I managed to read a few pages of. Not a book that I, or her, would normally read but it was distracting, and I resolved to read at least two pages a day. Which was a ridiculously tiny amount for me. But after a few days of doing this, I began to realise why reading fiction might be so hard. People had said that returning to book reading would be beneficial because I could lose myself in different stories, in different worlds, one of the positive things about a good book. However, the problem with losing yourself, even for a short moment, means that reality hits when you re-enter your real life and you get a rush of grief all-over again. And who would want that?

Along with my inability to read, I found I couldn't write either. I'd written an elegy for the funeral, and after that, it seemed I had no more words. Poetry turned out to be the way forwards, for both reading and for writing. I read a review on a book that had been written by the author following the death of her father. The words seemed to resonate, so I ordered a copy of *When the Tree Falls*, by Jane Clarke. I read it all, cried and empathised as her grief echoed my own. Her father had been a farmer, which made her poems seem more relevant to me, to us. I didn't want to wallow in other peoples' grief or my own, but her poems had sparked my lost interest in words so I grabbed the fragment of hope they offered and read more in a similar vein until one day, I was able to put into words my own feelings on loss.

On my bedside table is a copy of *One Long River of Song* by Brian Doyle, his posthumous collection of essays. I came upon his writing by chance and this book is now my go-to book whenever I don't know what to read. Or when things start to become difficult. I discovered that although fiction stayed a problem-read for me for a while, I was able to concentrate on non-fiction, particularly nature and place writing, maybe because I was able to stay in the same world. Doyle's writing in particular is evocative – descriptive, humorous, sad. I only found out halfway through reading this book that he died of the same brain tumour as

Dave. One of his essays is a letter addressed to his brother who had died two years previously. He wrote to his brother frequently and wanted to post one last one to him into the 'electrosphere'. It still brings tears to my eyes every time I read it, and I've read it many times. When Dave and I got together, in the days before mobile phones and emails, we used to write to each other. So I'm writing one last letter, and who knows, he might be able to read it.

When I moved, I found all the letters I'd written to you hibernating in a box. I started to read them but had to stop. They were too full of other peoples hopes and dreams. I've put them together with the ones you wrote to me. At least they'll be together.

I've heard others say that they'd give anything just to have one more day, one more hour, a minute with their loved one. We take things for granted when time isn't measured, don't we? As none of that is possible, I thought I'd write you this instead. It'll be the last one, I expect. And I will print it out and put it with the others, draw a line under them.

Your grandson is so tall now, but he hasn't changed much from the little boy that followed you around like one of the puppies. He always wanted to help you, be with you. Even though he's a teenager, he hasn't morphed into a monosyllabic being, not yet anyway.

Kim has done so well – you'd be so proud of her. I tell her this sometimes, but not too often as it makes her cry. And you know she doesn't like doing that. She'll finish her counselling degree this year – can you believe it? I can't. Some days we couldn't even get her out of bed to go to school. Her and Jordan are getting married this year, in the church near where you are. I can understand her wish to have it there, to be able to include you in some way, but the last time we were there was for your funeral so I'm not sure how I'm going to react. With grace and strength, I hope. After all, it's not about me.

Jasmine and James are still joined at the hip. I'm still so grateful that you were still here so you could go to their wedding. And although Letty is going through the terrible twos, she is a joy. At least you saw her first picture, even though it was just a scan. You carried that photo with you for weeks.

Hana and Nathan are fine and the babies that she never thought she'd have are doing so well. Twin boys and healthy, which is something we prayed for, after all the issues during her pregnancy. They are seven months old and so identical! Which sound ridiculous, but it's true. Luckily, their characters are already quite different, which is just as well as some days, I still have difficulty telling them apart, especially when she dresses them in the same clothes. You would have loved them – one has your name. They've already got their first rugby jerseys, although not in the colour you'd want.

I expect you know I've moved. Too many memories, and too much to do at the farm. I miss it, and you. I went back the other day and you're still there, in the fields and in the woods. Even in the kitchen, as the old oak beam that hold up the chimney probably still carries the marks of your head – you knocked it so many times. The silver birch that I planted in your memory is thriving, although it's been bark-stripped by the sheep. I figured you wouldn't mind that.

Life has moved on, but I haven't, not really. I'm still stuck in 'us' most days. I'm hoping that moving here will help, I try to concentrate on one day at a time. Or even an hour.

The window is open as I'm writing this. There's a hint of spring in the air – the first dusting of blackthorn flowers, the daffodils you always loved bending and dancing, a flush of green in the hedgerow. And I can hear a blackbird singing.

Other publications from the H'mm Foundation

Encounters with Nigel Jenkins
Edited by Jon Gower

CONTRIBUTORS:
Edwina Hart AM, John Barnie, Stevie Davies, Steve Griffiths, Angharad Jenkins and Branwen Jenkins, Noel Witts, Deborah Llewelyn, Robert Minhinnick, Peter Finch, John Davies, Menna Elfyn, Delyth Jenkins, Daniel G. Williams, Dave Hughes, Margo Morgan, Janet Dube, Jane James, Steve Griffiths, Ivor McGregor, Benjamin Palmer, Dave Oprava, Iwan Bala and Twm Morys, Janice Moore Fuller, Mike Parker and Ceri Wyn Jones, Ifor Thomas, Jane Fraser, Martyn Jenkins, Carey Knox, Steve Dube, Humberto Gatica, Tom Jenkins, D.J. Britton, Fflur Dafydd, Anne Lauppe-Dunbar, M. Wynn Thomas, Jon Gower and Peter Gruffydd.

ISBN 978-0-9927560-4-8

A Fiction Map of Wales
Edited by John Lavin

CONTRIBUTORS:
Rachel Trezise, Thomas Morris, Stevie Davies, Cynan Jones, Francesca Rhydderch, Joao Morais, Jon Gower, Rhian Elizabeth, Carly Holmes, Lloyd Jones, Gary Raymond, Tyler Keevil, Richard Redman, Georgia Carys Williams, Rhian Edwards, Rhys Milsom, Dic Edwards, Linda Ruhleman, Richard Gwyn, Kate Hamer and Robert Minhinnick.

ISBN 978-0-9927560-6-2

Encounters with R.S. Thomas
Edited by John Barnie

CONTRIBUTORS:
Gillian Clarke, Fflur Dafydd, Grahame Davies, Gwyneth Lewis, Peter Finch, Jon Gower, Menna Elfyn, Osi Rhys Osmond, Jeff Towns, Archbishop of Wales Barry Morgan, M. Wynn Thomas and First Minister of Scotland Alex Salmond.

ISBN 978-0-9927560-0-0

Encounters with Dylan Thomas
Edited by Jon Gower

CONTRIBUTORS:
Rachel Trezise, Michael Bogdanov, Kaite O'Reilly, D.J. Britton, Dafydd Elis-Thomas AM, Dai George, Sarah Gridley, Sarah King, Jeff Towns, George Tremlett, Steve Groves, Gary Raymond, Guy Masterson, Jon Gower, Horatio Clare and Andrew Lycett.

ISBN 978-0-9927560-2-4

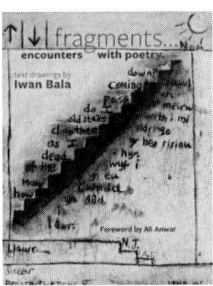  

It is as if... fragments
Essays about recent work by Iwan Bala, with images and DVD of the PROsiect hAlcw performances in collaboration with musician Angharad Jenkins, based on the poetry of her father, the late Nigel Jenkins.

CONTRIBUTORS:
Iwan Bala, Dr Anne Price-Owen, Osi Rhys Osmond, Twm Morys, Aneirin Karadog and Angharad Jenkins.

ISBN 978-0-9927560-8-6

Encounters with Osi
Essays about Osi Rhys Osmond, edited by Iwan Bala and Hilary Rhys Osmond.

CONTRIBUTORS:
Iwan Bala, Hilary Rhys Osmond, Ivor Davies, David Alston, M. Wynn Thomas, John Osmond, Christine Kinsey, Dai Smith, Karl Francis, Wyn Morris, David Parfitt, Mick and Thea Arnold, Hedley Jones, Noelle Francis, Susanne Schüeli, Teilo Trimble, Bella Kerr, Steve Wilson, Sam Vicary, Tina Carr, Siân Lewis, Nathan Osmond, Sara Rhys-Martin, Luke Osmond, Simon Thirsk, Lynne Crompton, Gwenan Rhys Price, Linda Sonntag, Rolf Jucker, Ché Osmond, Macsen Osmond, Colin Brewster, Ben Dressel, Megan Crofton, Lesley Davies, Beverley Oosthuizen-Jones, John Barnie, Menna Elfyn, Richard Pawelko and Mary Simmonds, Bethan John, Mererid Hopwood, Ann Oosthuizen,

ISBN 978-0-9927560-9-3

Encounters with John Selway
By Jon Gower

CONTRIBUTORS:
Paul Bowen, Derek Butler, Ivor Davies, Ken Elias, Richard Frame, Karl Francis, Brian Gardiner, Jonathan Glasbrook-Griffiths, Robert Alwyn Hughes, Alison Howard, David Hurn, Julian Meek, Phil Muirden, Osi Rhys Osmond, Brian Rice, Dai Smith, Marion Sprackling, Norman Toynton, Keith Underwood, Peter Wakelin, Phil Watkins, Roger and Den Wolfe.

ISBN 978-1-9999522-0-4

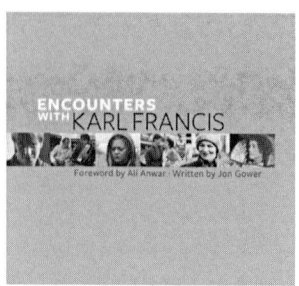

Encounters with Karl Francis

CONTRIBUTORS:
Foreword by Ali Anwar, written by Jon Gower

ISBN 978-1-9999522-1-1

Nigel Jenkins
Damned for Dreaming and other essays

CONTRIBUTORS:
Foreword by Ali Anwar and Jon Gower

ISBN 978-1-9999522-8-0

Osi Rhys Osmond
Cultural Alzheimers and other essays

CONTRIBUTORS:
Foreword by M. Wynn Thomas and Ali Anwar

ISBN 978-1-9999522-9-7

IMPACT*Ardrawiad*
Angharad Pearce Jones

Foreword by Ffion Rhys
Afterword by Ali Anwar

CONTRIBUTORS:
Dylan Huw, Beca Brown

ISBN 978-1-9999522-2-8

Shaping Art in Wales
Ceri Thomas

Foreword by Karen Mackinnon

ISBN 978-1-9999522-3-5

Wicked Words
£2.95

In partnership with The Wales Millenium Centre in 2015

ISBN 978-0-9927560-7-9

HON 2022
Artistiaid Benywaidd
Yng Nghymru
Women Artists In Wales

ARTISTIAID/ARTISTS
Marian Delyth
Sadia Pineda Hameed
Angharad Pearce Jones
Julia Griffiths Jones
Christine Kinsey
Sian Parri
Sarah Rhys
Catrin Webster
Sarah Williams
Sarah Younan

Editor Christine Kinsey
Introduction by Menna Elfyn and Ali Anwar

ISBN 978-1-9999522-6-6

Truth, Lies & Alibis
Encounters with
Christine Kinsey

Foreword by Ali Anwar and M. Wynn Thomas.
Introduction by Menna Elfyn

ISBN 978-1-9999522-5-9

The H'mm Foundation is:
c/o Bevan Buckland, Langdon House,
Langdon Road, Swansea SA1 8QY.
info@thehmmfoundation.co.uk
www.thehmmfoundation.co.uk